THE FOOD TRUCK COOKBOOK

A RANDOM HOUSE BOOK published by Random House New Zealand
18 Poland Road, Glenfield, Auckland, New Zealand

For more information about our titles go to www.randomhouse.co.nz

A catalogue record for this book is available from the National Library of New Zealand

Random House New Zealand is part of the Random House Group
New York   London   Sydney   Auckland   Delhi   Johannesburg

First published 2012. Reprinted 2012 (four times), 2013 (three times).

© 2012 text, Michael Van de Elzen, essay pp 88–91, André Taber, images Babiche Martens, except p. 88 and 89, Sir George Grey Special Collections, Auckland Libraries; p. 90, John Daley, Museum of New Zealand Te Papa Tongarewa; p. 91, New Zealand Herald, APN Holdings.

The moral rights of the authors have been asserted

ISBN 978 1 86979 837 6

Design: Kate Barraclough
Printed in New Zealand by Printlink

THE FOOD TRUCK COOKBOOK

Michael Van de Elzen

PHOTOS BY
BABICHE MARTENS

RANDOM HOUSE
NEW ZEALAND

Contents

A few words from Mike

IT WAS ANOTHER DRIZZLY WEEKEND, IN A SUMMER WHEN THE SUN JUST HADN'T SHONE NEARLY ENOUGH. I PULLED THE TRUCK OFF THE HIGHWAY JUST OUT OF WAIWERA, NORTH OF AUCKLAND, AND ONTO A BROAD STRIP OF GRASS WHERE, FOR AS LONG AS I CAN REMEMBER, THERE'S ALWAYS BEEN SOMEONE SELLING FOOD OUT OF THE BACK OF THE TRUCK OR VAN. ORANGES, STRAWBERRIES, SWEETCORN AND — ALMOST ALWAYS — FISH AND SHELLFISH.

I was feeling pretty anxious about the day ahead. Behind the cab, in the Food Truck kitchen, I had all sorts of fantastic seafood treats ready to go. I had bought everything fresh that morning and was intent on selling some of the most exciting seafood the fast-food market had ever seen. But in this persistent rain, I thought to myself, who's going to stop, get out of their car and check out the Food Truck offerings? Surely the traffic is just going to barrel on by?

I dragged the signboard out to the front of the truck and, in chalk, wrote 'Open'. It took about five minutes for the rain to wash off the words. 'Great', I muttered.

And then an amazing thing happened. Despite the low clouds, despite the fact that it was barely warm enough to be a shorts and T-shirt day, the cars started to slow down, pull over and turn onto the roadside strip. All of a sudden, I had a queue at the counter: surfer dudes on the way up to Mangawhai; families heading back home after their holidays; truck drivers in their big rigs — even a guy in a 4WD who drove off the road because he was so busy looking at us . . . They'd all recognised the truck from the first TV series and they were all keen to try my healthy fast food.

It was a far cry from my first time out in the truck a year before. That day I'd loaded up the truck with food I'd prepped in the kitchen of my Mount Eden restaurant, Molten, and headed down to the Auckland wharves to see if pie-loving truckies would rate my healthy, low-fat pie options. That day I truly thought I had gone crazy. Not only did I have a busy restaurant and bar to run, but my wife Belinda and I also had a three-month-old daughter who was waking several times a night and I was hard at work on my first book, *The Molten Cookbook*. You could say I had plenty on my plate.

But as I turned the key on the venerable 1970 Bedford and felt the engine roar — OK, splutter — into life, I knew that I had a job to do. My mission, which I'd enthusiastically chosen to accept, was to convince Kiwis that the fast food they loved could be healthy, fresh and taste great. And it was important they get that message because our love of takeaway food is one of the reasons for our *appalling* health statistics.

My mission, which I'd enthusiastically chosen to accept, was to convince Kiwis that the fast food they loved could be healthy, fresh and taste great.

Until I started *The Food Truck* I had no idea of the eye-watering statistics that lie behind the fast-food industry. For a start, it's worth $1.3 billion a year. Incredible! Then there's the volumes we munch through: 65 million pies a year. Astounding — and pretty horrifying, to be honest. And then there's the unhealthy ingredients it tends to contain: way too much fat, way too much salt, way too much MSG, way too much sugar and not nearly enough fibre. Yet we continue to load ourselves up with all this, even though fast food often doesn't even taste that great.

Don't get me wrong, I love fast food; at its best it's tasty, relatively affordable and convenient. I'm certainly guilty of chowing down on one too many Big Macs after a double shift at the restaurant, and I look back on every one of them with fond memories. We've always eaten takeaways in this country, as you will read in the essay

on the history of fast food in New Zealand further on in this book. But somewhere along the way we've begun eating them just a little bit too often.

Looking into our fast-food eating habits made me look at the way I cook as a chef, too. Restaurant kitchens typically turn out rich food, and being forced to use more vegetables, not use the deep fryer, and cut fat and sugar challenged me as a chef while making me realise how easy it is to make good, healthy food. It's made me ask myself, as a chef, is there another way? In the process it's opened up a whole new world of tastes, flavours and ingredients and given a new direction to my cooking.

The recipes in this book were all created in response to the challenges I put myself through in the TV series. I had less than a week to come up with each one, but this forced me to be creative and take chances with my food, something I think we should do every time we cook.

It wasn't always that simple to figure out what would work, and what could be churned out in high

I think one of the greatest things about the dishes in the following pages is that they were created with the help of everyday Kiwis, young and old, from all walks of life.

volumes at a fast pace, under the pressure of selling food at a large outdoor event. If you've seen the TV series, you'll know that even with great food I had mixed success. But it can be done, and it proved to me that there is another way.

I think one of the greatest things about the dishes in the following pages is that they were created with the help of everyday Kiwis, young and old, from all walks of life. It was so gratifying to see how people responded to the food I made. Not always, but for much of the time what I'd hoped for did eventuate: New Zealanders know great food when they see it and taste it — and they *will* buy it.

There will always be a time and place for fast food, but I hope that on the odd occasion rather than jumping in the car or picking up the phone, you open this cookbook. The recipes here are serious ones; they're not novelty, gimmicky dishes but rather creative, tasty, nourishing and appealing meals and snacks that you and your friends and family can enjoy. They are mostly easy to prepare. Most of all, they are

really delicious, and full of wonderful flavours that you perhaps didn't know could be there.

I hope the TV series and this book (with its per serving nutritional analyses) will help you think about the fast food you buy, how much you eat, when you eat it, and when you could cook it at home instead.

Quick Bites

Chips and dips

It's so much more rewarding to make your own corn chips. They are healthier as they are baked rather than deep-fried, and they just burst with true flavour. This recipe works only with fresh corn from the cob; canned or frozen corn will not do the trick.

Energy KJs	Protein	Total fat
1455	**16g**	**14g**

Saturated fat	Carbohy-drate	Sodium
2g	**43g**	**313mg**

Corn Chips
with red and green salsa

SERVES 4

1 x quantity tostada (see page 108)

1 x quantity red salsa (see Essentials, page 152)

1 x quantity green salsa (see Essentials, page 152)

FOR THE CORN CHIPS

1. Prepare tostada following recipe on page 108 up to step 4.
2. Cut cooked corn mixture into triangles.
3. Toast in preheated oven at 180°C for 3–4 minutes or until golden brown.
4. Cool and store in airtight container until needed.

FOR THE SALSAS

1. Prepare red and green salsas following the recipes in Essentials on page 152.

I wonder why we always buy potato chips when they're just so easy to make at home in the oven or microwave. When I served these at the kids' party all the kids loved them but wanted more flavour. I had to create that familiar chicken flavour without using any flavouring 621 (MSG) or artificial flavourings so often found in potato chips, so I overcooked some chicken and smashed it all up — the resulting flavour is awesome!

Energy KJs	Protein	Total fat
154	**4g**	**.18g**

Saturated fat	Carbohy-drate	Sodium
.04g	**23g**	**638mg**

Roasted Chips

SERVES 4

4 Agria potatoes, cut lengthwise into 3mm slices
salt and white pepper to taste
cooking oil spray

1. Preheat oven to 150°C. Spray a silicone baking sheet with oil.
2. Lightly season potato slices with salt and white pepper.
3. Spread out potatoes on baking sheet and spray tops with a little oil.
4. Bake for 20–25 minutes or until golden and crunchy.

Salt and vinegar seasoning

1 tablespoon sea salt
½ tablespoon cider vinegar

1. Combine salt and vinegar. Spread damp salt on a microwavable plate.
2. Microwave for 5 minutes until dry and crisp.
3. Store in an airtight container.

Chicken seasoning

1 skinless chicken breast, thinly sliced
olive oil spray
½ teaspoon garlic powder
½ teaspoon ground thyme
½ teaspoon ground rosemary
½ teaspoon sea salt
½ teaspoon white pepper

1. Preheat oven to 150°C.
2. Spray chicken slices with olive oil and place on a wire rack.
3. Bake for 35 minutes, or until dry and crisp.
4. Remove from oven and cool, then crush to a powder with a mortar and pestle.
5. Add garlic powder, thyme, rosemary and salt and pepper, and mix together.
6. Store in an airtight container.

Dehydrated vegetables are such a tasty alternative to the chips you might serve with dips. The hummus, cauliflower and lentil dips will see you star on the dip front, and the crispy kale leaves are extra special. The kale leaves are super nutritious, so if you can get the kids eating green chips then great, though I can't say I'm a convert just yet!

Energy KJs	Protein	Total fat
128	**1g**	**0g**

Saturated fat	Carbohydrate	Sodium
0g	**6g**	**43mg**

Dehydrated vegetable slices

SERVES 4

1 beetroot, cut into 3mm thick slices

1 carrot and parsnip, each cut lengthwise into 3mm thick slices

10cm cucumber, cut lengthwise into 3mm thick slices

1. Place vegetables in a dehydrator for 4 hours or until crisp.

OVEN METHOD

1. Preheat oven to 50°C.
2. Place vegetables on an oven tray and bake overnight.

Serve with roasted lemon hummus or cauliflower or lentil dips (see page 22).

Roasted lemon hummus

MAKES 2 CUPS

ROASTED LEMON

4 tablespoons water

½ tablespoon sugar

1 lemon, halved

HUMMUS

1 x 400g can chickpeas

1 roasted lemon, chopped

½ cup dry-roasted walnuts

2 tablespoons each toasted sunflower and pumpkin seeds

4 tablespoons water (approximately)

3 tablespoons olive oil

FOR THE ROASTED LEMON

1. Preheat oven to 150°C.
2. Heat an ovenproof frying pan to medium and add water, sugar and lemon halves. Stir until sugar is dissolved.
3. Bake for 15–20 minutes or until lemon is soft. Remove and season with salt and pepper.

FOR THE HUMMUS

1. Place drained and rinsed chickpeas and roasted lemon in a food processor and blend until smooth.
2. Crush walnuts and seeds and add to food processor.
3. With the motor running, gradually add enough water until the mixture becomes a thick purée. Add olive oil and process until blended.

Cauliflower dip

MAKES 2 CUPS

1 small head cauliflower, cut into florets
olive oil spray
2 soft-boiled eggs, peeled
½ cup vegetable stock
4 tablespoons olive oil
1 tablespoon smoked oil (available from specialty food stores)
salt and ground black pepper to taste

1. Preheat oven to 150°C.
2. Cook cauliflower in a saucepan of lightly salted boiling water until tender. Drain.
3. Spray cauliflower with olive oil and place in a baking dish. Season to taste.
4. Bake for about 15 minutes or until starting to colour. Remove from oven and cool.
5. Place cauliflower in a blender or food processor. Add eggs and stock, and process for 10 seconds. Scrape down sides of blender and, while motor is running, gradually add oils. Season with salt and pepper.

Lentil dip

MAKES 4 CUPS

3 cups cooked Puy lentils
3 Roma tomatoes, finely chopped
1 tablespoon parsley, finely chopped
8 cloves garlic, roasted and crushed
3 tablespoons olive oil
pinch each salt and white pepper

1. Mix lentils, tomatoes, parsley and garlic together in a bowl. Add olive oil, season with salt and pepper and mix well.
2. Place half the mixture in a food processor and blend until smooth.
3. Fold processed mixture back into remaining lentils.

Crispy kale leaves

1 bunch kale, leaves only, torn into bite-sized pieces
olive oil for sprinkling
salt to taste

1. Preheat oven to 175°C.
2. Sprinkle kale leaves with olive oil and salt and toss.
3. Place on a silicone baking sheet on an oven tray.
4. Bake for 10 minutes until crisp.

The Classics

*Pies, burgers
and pizzas*

When I went out to see Eddie at Dad's Pies, they told me a vegetable pie will never sell. I showed them! This fantastic-tasting pie sold like hot cakes. It's really easy and even the pastry is low in fat.

Energy KJs	Protein	Total fat
3114	**16g**	**48g**

Saturated fat	Carbohydrate	Sodium
9g	**62g**	**317mg**

vegetable pie

SERVES 4

PASTRY

2½ cups wholemeal flour

2 teaspoons turmeric

¾ cup olive oil

2 teaspoons cider vinegar

¾ cup cold water

VEGETABLE FILLING

4 tablespoons cooked chickpeas

4 tablespoons cooked black beans

2 cups loosely packed baby spinach leaves

50g ricotta

1 cup diced dry-roasted pumpkin

1 clove garlic, crushed

½ cup cooked or canned green lentils, drained and mashed

½ cup lite coconut milk

pepper to taste

½ teaspoon curry powder

2 teaspoons grated Parmesan

1. Preheat oven to 180°C. Spray 4 x 10cm pie dishes or 4 large muffin pans with a little oil.
2. Place flour and turmeric in a bowl. Add olive oil and combine until mixture resembles breadcrumbs.
3. Mix cider vinegar and water together and add to flour mixture to form a dough.
4. Sprinkle flour on a large board and roll out dough to 2.5mm thick. Cut bases to fit the pie dishes or muffin pans and then line. Cut tops to fit and set aside.
5. Mix all filling ingredients together in a bowl.
6. Spoon filling into pastry cases.
7. Moisten top edge of pastry with a little water. Place pastry lid on top of mixture, and press down to join edges.
8. Bake for 25 minutes, or until pastry is golden.

We all grew up eating our mums' great fish pies. It's a real Kiwi dish. I used bread dough instead of pastry; it gives greater bulk, to fill you up, and it really reduces the fat content. It's easier than making pastry, too.

Energy KJs	Protein	Total fat
1544	**17g**	**8g**

Saturated fat	Carbohydrate	Sodium
1.4g	**58g**	**420mg**

Fish pie

SERVES 4

WHOLEMEAL DOUGH

130ml warm water

1 tablespoon olive oil

2 teaspoons sugar

pinch salt

1 teaspoon dried yeast

200g wholemeal flour

100g white flour

SMOKED KAWAHAI FILLING

½ side smoked kahawai

½ cup low-fat milk

½ onion and ½ leek, diced

1 clove garlic, crushed

olive oil for sautéing

1 cup frozen peas

1 teaspoon cornflour

1 tablespoon wholegrain mustard

white pepper to taste

SALSA

1 teaspoon each chopped gherkin
    and capers

1 boiled egg, white only, chopped

1 tablespoon each chopped parsley
    and coriander

1 teaspoon olive oil

FOR THE DOUGH

1. Place warm water, olive oil, sugar and salt in a warm bowl and stir to dissolve sugar. Sprinkle yeast over mixture and continue stirring to blend in yeast. Stir in wholemeal flour and half the white flour, or sufficient to make a thick batter. Beat until smooth. Add remaining flour and mix to form a dough.

2. Turn out onto a board and knead for about 10 minutes until dough is smooth. Place dough in a bowl sprayed with oil and turn over to coat all sides. Cover with plastic film and leave to rise in a warm place until doubled in bulk.

3. After dough has risen, punch down and roll into a ball. Set aside.

FOR THE FILLING

1. Preheat oven to 180°C. Skin kahawai and tear into large chunks.

2. Place milk in a saucepan, add kahawai and simmer until just heated through. Remove fish and keep warm. Reserve milk.

3. In another pan, sauté onion, leek and garlic in olive oil until soft. Add reserved milk and peas, and cook for 2–3 minutes. Mix cornflour with a little water and add to mixture. Cook until thickened. Add fish and mustard, season with pepper and combine.

4. Roll out dough and cut into 4 x 20cm rounds. Spoon fish mixture into the middle of the dough. Pinch sides together to form a case.

5. Bake on a greased tray for 15–20 minutes until case is golden brown.

FOR THE SALSA

1. Mix all ingredients together. Remove pies from oven and sprinkle with salsa. Garnish with baby cress.

This one's a classic Kiwi pie, the nation's favourite type of pie, and it's no surprise that I sold more of this than any other during the pie challenge. I used rump steak, which is an affordable cut, and the vegetable topping makes it a meal in itself. Using potato top on any pie is a great way to reduce the amount of pastry used but still keep that delicious flavour.

Energy KJs	Protein	Total fat
1534	**19g**	**20g**

Saturated fat	Carbohydrate	Sodium
7g	**25g**	**177mg**

steak and cheese pie

SERVES 4

STEAK FILLING

4 x 10cm precooked vol au vent cases
½ onion, sliced
½ clove garlic, crushed
250g rump steak, sliced into 1cm thick strips
2 Portobello mushrooms, sliced
½ teaspoon Dijon mustard
12 cherry tomatoes

TOPPING

1 cup cooked potato
3 tablespoons olive oil
3 tablespoons low-fat milk
white pepper to taste
1 teaspoon grated Parmesan

1. Preheat grill. Warm vol au vent cases.
2. Heat a heavy-based frying pan. Spray with oil and add onion and garlic. Stir-fry for 1–2 minutes. Then add beef strips, mushrooms and mustard and stir-fry for a further 2–3 minutes. Add tomatoes and combine. Set aside.
3. Mash potato with olive oil, milk and pepper, and place in a piping bag. Set aside.
4. Pile steak mixture into warm vol au vent cases. Pipe potato on top of each pie and sprinkle with Parmesan.
5. Grill until potato is golden.

EDDIE OF DAD'S PIES

Dad's Pies in Silverdale has some of the most advanced equipment I've ever seen in a bakery. It's on the cutting edge of pie making. Eddie is really passionate about what he makes and genuinely cares about his products and his staff. He limits them to eating one pie a day! He didn't have much faith in the sales prospects for my vegetarian pie but he did say to me after I told him how well it sold that he might have to get me to give him the recipe.
Watch this space!

This is the classic thin-crust pizza. If you don't have a pizza oven, try cooking the pizza on a pizza stone on your barbecue with the heat cranked up as hot as it will go. A really high temperature is the key to pizza success!

Energy KJs	Protein	Total fat
1129	**12g**	**8g**

Saturated fat	Carbohydrate	Sodium
2g	**37g**	**375mg**

margherita pizza

MAKES 2 BASES, SERVES 4

WHOLEMEAL PIZZA DOUGH

150g white flour

50g wholemeal flour

pinch salt

60ml low-fat milk

60ml water

7g dried yeast

¼ teaspoon sugar

TOPPING

½ cup tomato sauce (see Essentials, page 152)

50g buffalo mozzarella

2 tablespoons basil

FOR THE DOUGH

1. Sift together white and wholemeal flours and salt, and leave in a warm place.
2. Gently heat milk and water to blood temperature, then add yeast and sugar. Leave in a warm place for yeast to activate and bubble.
3. Add liquid ingredients to dry and mix to form a dough. Turn out onto a board and knead by hand, or in a mixer, until smooth. Place dough in an oiled bowl, cover and leave in a warm place to double in size.
4. Knead again and rest for 20 minutes before using.
5. Sprinkle flour onto a board. Divide dough in half and roll out as thinly as possible into 2 pizza bases.

FOR THE TOPPING

1. Preheat oven to 180°C. Place baking trays in oven to heat.
2. Spread tomato sauce on both bases and top with mozzarella. Place on hot trays.
3. Bake in preheated oven until base is crisp and lightly browned.
4. Arrange basil on top and serve.

Kiwis love meat pizzas — here's one that's low fat. Venison is extremely lean, an ideal substitute for the fat- and preservative-heavy dried meats of so many takeaway meat-lovers' pizzas. You could also use lean lamb or lean beef (just make sure you wash off all the salt!).

Energy KJs	Protein	Total fat
1752	**18g**	**14g**

Saturated fat	Carbohydrate	Sodium
4g	**55g**	**605mg**

venison pizza
with mushrooms, onion jam and rocket salsa verde

MAKES 2 BASES, SERVES 4

VENISON

1 teaspoon sea salt

200g venison medallions, trimmed of excess fat

1 tablespoon peppercorns

1 tablespoon ground juniper berries

1 tablespoon ground cumin

SMOKED MUSHROOMS

1 cup untreated sawdust for smoking

4 large Portobello mushrooms

ROCKET SALSA VERDE

1 handful rocket, finely chopped

½ teaspoon mustard

1 teaspoon olive oil

zest of ½ lemon

1 teaspoon capers, drained and finely diced

¼ avocado, finely diced

½ clove garlic, finely diced

FOR THE VENISON

1. Sprinkle a small amount of sea salt over venison, then sprinkle with peppercorns, juniper and cumin. Place on a tray that will collect the salt liquids. Cover and place in refrigerator overnight.
2. Next day, wash venison. Heat a frying pan to high and seal and colour venison. Roll in plastic wrap to set shape. Set aside and cool.

FOR THE SMOKED MUSHROOMS

1. Preheat oven to 180°C. Place some untreated sawdust in the bottom of a baking dish.
2. Roll some aluminium foil into four balls, place on sawdust and place a mushroom, gill side down, on top of each. Cover dish with foil.
3. Bake for about 5 minutes or until smoke fills the dish.

FOR THE ROCKET SALSA VERDE

1. Mix all ingredients together.

Recipe continued over page…

Venison pizza continued…

TO ASSEMBLE

2 wholemeal pizza bases (see page 34)

3 tablespoons tomato sauce (see Essentials, page 152)

3 tablespoons onion jam (see Essentials, page 149)

100g smoked mushrooms, sliced

40g pecorino, grated

50g venison

3 tablespoons rocket salsa verde

50g snow pea shoots or other microgreens

TO ASSEMBLE

1. Preheat oven to 200°C. Place baking trays in oven to heat up.
2. Spread both bases with tomato sauce and onion jam. Top with mushrooms and half the pecorino. Place on hot trays.
3. Bake until base is crisp and lightly browned.
4. Slice venison very thinly and place on pizzas. Top with salsa verde and finish with remaining pecorino and snow pea shoots.

This one's a bit different. Pomegranate seeds give that wonderful, poppy burst of sweet pomegranate juice when you bite into them. This, with the earthiness of the lentils, makes this pizza a fabulous dish even for non-vegetarians.

Energy KJs	Protein	Total fat
1577	**15g**	**12g**

Saturated fat	Carbohydrate	Sodium
4g	**53g**	**731mg**

Vegetarian pizza

SERVES 4

6 tablespoons tomato sauce (see Essentials, page 152)

2 wholemeal pizza bases (see page 34)

1 cup cooked lentils

2 cups spinach leaves

40g goat's cheese

40g ricotta

1 pomegranate, seeds and juice

½ teaspoon olive oil

6 wild rocket leaves

1. Preheat oven to 180°C. Place baking trays in oven to heat up.
2. Spread tomato sauce on bases and scatter over lentils. Top with spinach leaves, goat's cheese and ricotta. Place on hot trays.
3. Bake until bases are crisp and lightly browned.
4. Mix pomegranate seeds (if you use dried pomegranate seeds, you will need to soak them first to plump them up) and juice with oil. Drizzle pomegranate dressing over pizzas, garnish with rocket, and serve.

It is big! Getting lots of vegetables into the patty not only makes it a lot healthier, but it bulks it up while also making it light. Beetroot is the quintessential Kiwi burger ingredient, and here I use it to give real colour to the patty.

Energy KJs	Protein	Total fat
2339	**41g**	**28g**

Saturated fat	Carbohydrate	Sodium
7g	**42g**	**580mg**

Big mike's
beef and veggie burgers

SERVES 4

PATTIES

500g premium lean beef mince

1 onion, finely diced

1 courgette, grated

½ beetroot, grated

1 teaspoon Dijon mustard

½ teaspoon curry powder (cumin, coriander, chilli)

3 egg whites

MIKE'S AWESOME SAUCE

2 soft-boiled eggs

4 shallots, sliced and sautéed

1 tablespoon honey

1 tablespoon tomato purée

100ml vegetable stock

60ml olive oil

2 gherkins, finely chopped

TO ASSEMBLE

4 wholemeal buns

2 heads baby cos lettuce, finely sliced

4 gherkins, each sliced into 4

FOR THE PATTIES

1. Preheat oven to 180°C.
2. Mix all ingredients together in a bowl. Form into 8 patties.
3. Heat a heavy-based frying pan until hot and brown the patties on both sides. Place on a baking tray.
4. Bake for 4–5 minutes.

FOR THE SAUCE

1. Boil eggs in boiling water for 5 minutes exactly, then run under cold water until cold. Peel carefully.
2. Place eggs, shallots, honey, tomato purée and stock in a food processor. Process to combine. With the motor running, gradually add oil while processing to form an emulsion.
3. Remove from food processor and add gherkins. Set aside.

Slice buns into 3. Add Mike's Awesome Sauce, pattie, lettuce and gherkin on each bun base. Repeat with a second pattie on each bun middle. Finish with bun tops.

I smoked the chicken for these patties, which gave it an amazing flavour. If you don't have a smoker or don't want to smoke it, then cooking it on an open flame on the barbecue is just as good.

Energy KJs	Protein	Total fat
2004	**28g**	**21g**

Saturated fat	Carbohydrate	Sodium
4g	**44g**	**228mg**

Chicken burgers

SERVES 4

WHOLEMEAL BUNS

130ml warm water

1 tablespoon olive oil

2 teaspoons sugar

pinch salt

8g fresh yeast

200g wholemeal flour

100g white flour

100g kumara, peeled, roasted and
  mashed

SMOKED CHICKEN

4 boneless, skinless chicken thighs

1 teaspoon Dijon mustard

1 cup untreated sawdust for
  smoking

FOR THE BUNS

1. Place warm water, olive oil, sugar and salt in a warm bowl and stir to dissolve sugar. Sprinkle yeast over mixture and continue stirring to blend in yeast. Stir in wholemeal flour and half the white flour, or sufficient to make a thick batter. Beat until smooth. Add kumara and remaining flour and mix to form a dough.

2. Turn out onto a board and knead for about 10 minutes until dough is smooth.

3. Place dough in a bowl sprayed with oil and turn over to coat all sides. Cover with plastic film and leave to rise in a warm place until doubled in bulk.

4. After dough has risen, punch down, knead again and form dough into 4 buns. Leave to double in size. Preheat oven to 180°C. Place buns on a baking tray.

5. Bake for about 12 minutes.

FOR THE CHICKEN

1. Brush chicken thighs with mustard. Cover and leave in refrigerator for about 15 minutes to allow flavours to penetrate.

2. Place some untreated sawdust in a heavy-based pan, then place a rack on top of the pan. Put chicken on the rack and cover pan with aluminium foil and then a lid.

3. Place pan on element, turn heat to high and leave until smoke appears. Then turn off heat and leave for 8 minutes.

4. Heat a ridged pan to hot. Cook smoked chicken for 2–3 minutes each side. Remove and cool.

Recipe continued over page…

Chicken burgers continued…

TZATZIKI

½ telegraph cucumber, deseeded
and cut into matchsticks

2 teaspoons chopped mint

4 tablespoons plain unsweetened
yoghurt

½ teaspoon lemon juice

TO ASSEMBLE

4 tablespoons aubergine pickle (see
Essentials, page 150)

¼ cup alfalfa sprouts

4 tablespoons tomato sauce (see
Essentials, page 152)

FOR THE TZATZIKI

1. Mix all ingredients together.

Slice buns in half and spread base with aubergine pickle. Slice each chicken thigh in half on the diagonal and place on pickle. Add a dollop of tzatziki, then finish with alfalfa sprouts, tomato sauce and bun top.

This burger has such a burstingly great combo of flavour, texture and nutrition that any meat eater would want to grab it. Not only that but quinoa and buckwheat are just packed full of goodness.

Energy KJs	Protein	Total fat
2980	**22g**	**23g**

Saturated fat	Carbohy- drate	Sodium
6g	**117g**	**468mg**

vegetarian burgers

SERVES 4

ALMOND SATAY SAUCE

1 teaspoon vegetable oil

½ onion, finely chopped

½ clove garlic, crushed

1 teaspoon finely chopped fresh ginger

1 teaspoon curry powder

1 teaspoon low-sodium soy sauce

200ml lite coconut milk

¼ cup almond butter

BEETROOT PICKLE

1 cup white wine vinegar or cider vinegar

½ cup sugar

1 star anise

1 cinnamon quill

2 cups grated beetroot

FOR THE SAUCE

1. Heat a heavy-based frying pan, add oil and sauté onion until transparent. Add garlic, ginger and curry powder and cook for 1–2 minutes.
2. Add soy sauce and coconut milk and simmer for 10 minutes. Stir in almond butter until well blended.

FOR THE PICKLE

1. Place vinegar, sugar, star anise and cinnamon quill in a saucepan and heat until reduced by half. The mixture will be thick and sticky. Remove star anise and cinnamon quill.
2. Add beetroot and cook, stirring, for 2–3 minutes.

Recipe continued over page…

Vegetarian burgers continued…

PUMPKIN AND SPINACH PATTIES

2 onions, sliced and sautéed

¼ cup buckwheat

¼ cup cooked quinoa

¼ cup cooked chickpeas

¼ cup lite coconut milk

¼ cup almonds, dry roasted

1 carrot, grated

1 cup roasted, diced pumpkin

1 cup baby spinach leaves

½ teaspoon thyme leaves

½ teaspoon lemon juice

1 tablespoon chopped parsley

3 egg whites

TO ASSEMBLE

4 wholemeal buns (see recipe on
  page 44)

8 lettuce leaves

snow pea sprouts

¼ cup alfalfa sprouts

FOR THE PATTIES

1. Mix all ingredients together in a bowl. Form into 4 patties.
2. Heat a heavy-based frying pan and spray with a little oil. Cook patties until golden on both sides.

Slice buns in half and spread almond satay sauce on each base. Add lettuce and top with a pattie. Then spoon on beetroot pickle and finish with snow pea shoots, alfalfa sprouts and bun top.

peter of the white lady

The White Lady is an Auckland institution — it's been serving food for over 60 years, so taking it on was going to be my biggest challenge. Parking up behind their truck late at night and starting the clock for a burger-off, it soon became clear the young patrons of the night were not interested in my healthy versions. They preferred size, and lashings of fat. However, after my wiping, Peter asked for my chicken burger recipe. I believe that burger is still on the menu. That's flippin' awesome!

Fishy Business

*Sliders, shots
and seadogs*

*OK, so one gentleman thought the burger lacked mussel, but I stand by this recipe
as a great fritter or patty recipe that everyone will love, even those who are a bit
scared of mussels. I had planned to make these sliders for the TV show episode but
the burger buns came back too big so I had to do normal size burgers. Here's the
way I had originally intended them…*

Energy KJs	Protein	Total fat
1533	**24g**	**4.5g**

Saturated fat	Carbohydrate	Sodium
1g	**58g**	**1040mg**

mussel sliders

SERVES 4, 3 SLIDERS EACH

MUSSEL FRITTERS

½ cup rice flour

½ cup chickpea flour

1 teaspoon baking soda

pinch salt

2 teaspoons smoked paprika

2 large shallots, finely diced

½ cup water

2 cups cooked mussels, chopped

TO ASSEMBLE

8–12 cos lettuce leaves

1–2 tomatoes, sliced

12 small wholemeal dinner rolls

1 cup raisin chutney (see Essentials,
   page 149)

FOR THE FRITTERS

1. Mix together dry ingredients in a bowl. Add shallots and water, and stir to form a thin batter. Add a little more water if necessary. Then add mussels and combine.

2. Heat a heavy-based frying pan and spray with a little oil. Pour a tablespoon of the mixture in the pan, and repeat with remaining mixture to make four fritters. Cook until golden, then turn and cook the other side.

*Place lettuce and tomato on bun bases, add fritters, top with chutney, and finish
with bun tops.*

This recipe is me tipping my hat to New Zealand's first fast-food outlets — the oyster saloons that were common in the nineteenth century, as the history on page 88 notes.
The order to eat this in is: oyster, tomato, salad. You will just love the colour the avocado oil gives to this dish, and being an unsaturated oil it's so good for you.

Energy KJs **787**	Protein **4g**	Total fat **17g**
Saturated fat **3g**	Carbohy-drate **5g**	Sodium **346mg**

Oysters with tomato horseradish shooter
and witloof, celery and avocado salad

SERVES 6

WITLOOF, CELERY AND AVOCADO SALAD

1 avocado, diced
¼ telegraph cucumber, deseeded and peeled into ribbons
2 stalks celery, diced
3 tablespoons avocado oil
pinch salt
white pepper to taste
6 witloof leaves

TOMATO SHOOTER

3 medium tomatoes, roughly chopped
1 cup tomato juice
1 tablespoon horseradish cream
pinch salt
white pepper to taste

6 oysters in the half-shell
lemon wedges for garnish

FOR THE SALAD

1. Combine avocado, cucumber, celery, oil and salt and pepper, and toss.
2. Spoon salad into witloof leaves.

FOR THE SHOOTER

1. Place tomatoes, tomato juice, horseradish cream, salt and pepper in a blender and process until smooth.
2. Chill then pour into shot glasses.

Serve shooters alongside an oyster and filled witloof leaf. Garnish with a small lemon wedge.

This is a dish I'd happily serve in a restaurant, and it's got so much less fat than standard fish and chips. Coating the fish with Dijon mustard gives it heaps of flavour and helps the crumbs to stick. Kumara makes a nice change from potato when you are making chips.

Energy KJs	Protein	Total fat
2943	**28g**	**37g**

Saturated fat	Carbohydrate	Sodium
6g	**64g**	**828mg**

Crumbed fish and kumara chips
with pepperanato purée

SERVES 4

PEPPERANATO PURÉE

1 tablespoon olive oil

3 onions, peeled and finely sliced

2 cloves garlic, crushed

500g Roma tomatoes, blanched, refreshed, skinned and cut into quarters

4 red peppers, chargrilled, skinned, deseeded and thinly sliced

1 handful fresh basil

pinch salt

freshly ground black pepper to taste

KUMARA CHIPS

4 kumara, cut into chunky chips

3 tablespoons olive oil

pinch each salt and white pepper

CRUMBED FISH

3 tablespoons olive oil

½ loaf wholemeal bread, processed into breadcrumbs

pinch each salt and white pepper

4 x 100g fillets snapper

2 teaspoons Dijon mustard

FOR THE PURÉE

1. Heat olive oil a heavy-based saucepan. Add onions and garlic and sweat until onions are translucent. Add tomato quarters, then add sliced peppers and cook for 2–3 minutes or until most of the liquid has evaporated. Add basil and purée with a stick blender or in a food processor. Season with salt and pepper.

FOR THE CHIPS

1. Preheat oven to 180°C. Line a baking tray with baking paper.
2. Place kumara chips in a bowl, drizzle with olive oil and sprinkle with salt and pepper. Mix to coat chips. Lay chips in a single layer on the baking tray.
3. Bake for 10–12 minutes or until tender and golden.

FOR THE FISH

1. Line a baking tray with a silicone baking sheet.
2. Heat olive oil in a heavy-based pan. Add breadcrumbs, salt and pepper and sauté for 3–5 minutes or until crisp.
3. Brush top side of snapper with mustard. Then pat crisp breadcrumbs onto mustard. Place snapper on baking tray.
4. Bake in preheated oven for 5 minutes.

Serve with a lemon wedge.

Incredibly easy, this is a great dish to get your kids to help you make, or make themselves. You'll need to use a Japanese turning machine to slice the potatoes that finely; you can find them in most Asian food stores. You can make these on the barbecue, too.

Energy KJs **1284**	Protein **41g**	Total fat **7g**
Saturated fat **2g**	Carbohydrate **20g**	Sodium **144mg**

curly wurlies
with pea purée

SERVES 4

CURLY WURLIES

720g snapper fillets, cut into
  12 x 60g strips
4 potatoes, peeled and cut into
  strings on a Japanese turning
  machine or citrus peeler
canola oil for spraying

PEA PURÉE

1 cup frozen peas
white pepper to taste

FOR THE CURLY WURLIES

1. Preheat oven to 180°C.
2. Wrap strips of fish in potato strings, then spray wrapped fish with canola oil. Place in a baking dish.
3. Bake for 3 minutes on each side.

FOR THE PEA PURÉE

1. Boil peas until just cooked. Drain, cool immediately and process in a food processor until puréed. Season with pepper.

Thread a skewer through the curly wurlies and serve with the pea purée.

Baking fish in paper locks in all the flavours of the fish and keeps it moist. You can package them up ahead of time and have them sitting in the fridge until you need them. Cook them in the oven or on the barbecue. And no dishes!

Energy KJs	Protein	Total fat
743	**21g**	**9g**

Saturated fat	Carbohy-drate	Sodium
2g	**4g**	**247mg**

paper-baked fish
with salsa verde

SERVES 4

FISH

4 x 100g snapper fillets
1 bulb fennel, sliced thinly
1 teaspoon olive oil
pinch salt
ground black pepper to taste
4 teaspoons lite crème fraîche
¼ teaspoon lemon juice

SALSA VERDE

½ tablespoon chopped capers
½ tablespoon chopped gherkin
1 tablespoon chopped parsley
1 tablespoon avocado oil
1 tablespoon chopped watercress
1 teaspoon grated Parmesan

lemon or lime wedges for garnish

FOR THE FISH

1. Preheat oven to 180°C.
2. Place each portion of fish on a square of baking paper. Top with fennel slices. Drizzle with olive oil and season with salt and pepper. Wrap paper over fish to make a parcel. Place parcels on a baking tray.
3. Bake for 12 minutes.
4. Mix crème fraîche and lemon juice together.

FOR THE SALSA

1. Mix all ingredients together in a bowl.

Drizzle salsa over the fish and serve with a dollop of crème fraîche. If you have a lime or lemon handy, cut a wedge and squeeze the juice over.

This recipe makes 20 sausages; you can freeze the extras. You will need to make the sausage mixture as moist as possible so it's pliable. Keep it cold, too, which will stop the ingredients from separating. If you don't like paua, or don't have it, use pork or chicken instead. Gribiche is a sort of tartare sauce without the mayo, making it so much healthier.

Energy KJs	Protein	Total fat
3830	**65g**	**50g**

Saturated fat	Carbohydrate	Sodium
9g	**51g**	**776mg**

seadogs in a bun
with horseradish mayonnaise and dry gribiche

SERVES 4

WHOLEGRAIN AND CHIA SEED BUNS

Makes 4

150g white flour
50g wholegrains, e.g. oats
½ cup chia seeds
pinch salt
60ml low-fat milk
60ml water
7g dried yeast
¼ teaspoon sugar

DRY GRIBICHE

3 hard-boiled eggs, diced
1 shallot, diced
½ tablespoon capers, drained and chopped
2 gherkins, finely diced
½ teaspoon lemon zest
1 tablespoon chopped parsley
white pepper to taste

FOR THE BUNS

1. Sift white flour in a bowl and combine with wholegrains, chia seeds and salt. Leave bowl in a warm place.
2. Gently heat milk and water to blood temperature. Add yeast and sugar, and leave in a warm place for yeast to activate and bubble.
3. Add wet ingredients to dry and mix to form a dough. Turn out onto a board and knead by hand, or in a mixer, until smooth. Place in an oiled bowl, cover and leave in a warm place to double in size.
4. Preheat oven to 220°C.
5. Punch down dough, knead again and shape into 4 buns. Leave to double in size. Place buns on a baking tray.
6. Bake for about 12 minutes.

FOR THE GRIBICHE

1. Mix all ingredients together.

Recipe continued over page…

Seadogs in a bun continued…

HORSERADISH MAYONNAISE
1 teaspoon grated fresh horseradish
1 egg yolk
1 teaspoon white wine vinegar
½ teaspoon Dijon mustard
100ml rice bran oil

SEADOGS (PAUA SAUSAGES)
Makes 20
200ml low-fat milk
½ onion, studded with
  10 whole cloves
½ teaspoon nutmeg
½ teaspoon allspice
70g fresh breadcrumbs
375g chicken mince
1 egg white
2 tablespoons milk
250g paua, minced
250g pickled pork
½ teaspoon white pepper
1 sausage casing

FOR THE MAYONNAISE
1. Place horseradish, egg yolk, vinegar and mustard in a food processor and process to combine. With the motor running, gradually add oil until thick and blended.

FOR THE SEADOGS
1. Place milk in a saucepan and bring to the boil, then add clove-studded onion. Reduce heat and simmer until liquid reduces by two-thirds. Remove onion, and stir in nutmeg and allspice. Pour milk into a bowl and mix in breadcrumbs. Set aside.
2. Place chicken in a blender, add egg white and blend. Remove and place mixture in a bowl over ice (to keep the mixture cool) and gently beat in 2 tablespoons of milk. The mixture should be smooth and glossy.
3. Blend paua and pork together then add to chicken mousse. Squeeze out breadcrumbs, reserving milk, and add to chicken and paua mixture. Season with pepper.
4. Fill sausage skins with mixture.
5. Pour reserved milk into a saucepan and add an equal amount of water. Bring to a simmer and gently poach sausages for 20 minutes. Do not let the temperature of the liquid rise above 90°C.

If necessary, reheat sausages by simmering in milk. Cut each bun almost in half. Place one seadog in each bun and top with horseradish mayo and dry gribiche.

The ultimate one-pot seafood wonder. You can mix and match any seafood you have and it will still taste fantastic. You'll love it!

Energy KJs	Protein	Total fat
1265	**24g**	**13g**

Saturated fat	Carbohydrate	Sodium
3g	**23g**	**544mg**

orzo paella
with watercress salsa

SERVES 6

WATERCRESS SALSA

3 tablespoons chopped watercress
zest of ½ lemon
2 tablespoons avocado oil
pinch salt
white pepper to taste

PAELLA

2 medium-sized chorizo, sliced
6 shallots, sliced
3 cloves garlic, finely chopped
300g fresh squid, cleaned, scored and sliced
200g monkfish fillets, finely sliced
1 teaspoon smoked paprika
3 tomatoes, diced
12 surf clams or cockles
1 cup fish stock
3 cups cooked orzo
3 courgettes, sliced into 4mm strips
drizzle olive oil
pinch salt and white pepper
½ head radicchio, sliced

FOR THE SALSA

1. Combine all ingredients.

FOR THE PAELLA

1. Heat a large heavy-based saucepan to hot and spray with a little oil.
2. Add chorizo and sauté until golden. Add shallots, garlic, squid and monkfish and sauté for about 1 minute. Add smoked paprika and stir to combine, then mix in tomatoes, clams and fish stock.
3. Cover and shake pan. Continue cooking for 3–4 minutes, regularly shaking pan until all clams have opened.
4. Add orzo, stirring to combine, and heat thoroughly.
5. Drizzle courgettes with a little olive oil and season with pinch of salt and white pepper. Char on hot barbecue or griddle pan.
6. Add courgettes and radicchio to pan and stir through.

Serve orzo paella garnished with watercress salsa.

meaty matters

Kebabs, chicken and brisket sandwich

These skewers are great to roast or just throw on the barbecue. Eat them hot out of the oven, or let them cool down and eat them for lunch or on a picnic. Add the apples to the chow chow when you serve it to keep them crisp and stop them colouring. The recipes here are for separate vegetable and pork kebabs but for the photo I've threaded them together. Over to you which you prefer!

Energy KJs	Protein	Total fat
190	**1.7g**	**.6g**

Saturated fat	Carbohy-drate	Sodium
0g	**8g**	**99mg**

kebabs
Roast vegetable kebabs

MAKES 12

2 parsnips, peeled and cut into chunks

4 courgettes, trimmed and cut into chunks

2 swedes, peeled and cut into chunks

2 beetroot, peeled and cut into chunks

12 skewers, soaked in cold water

1. Preheat oven to 170°C.
2. Heat an ovenproof pan and spray with a little oil. Add parsnips and sauté until lightly browned. Set aside and repeat with other vegetables, sautéing each vegetable separately.
3. Place vegetables in separate oven dishes and roast in preheated oven for about 12 minutes, except for courgettes, which only need 6 minutes.
4. Remove vegetables from oven and increase temperature to 180°C.
5. Place vegetable chunks on skewers when cool enough to handle. Place skewers in an oven dish. Return kebabs to the oven and roast for 10 minutes.

Serve with apple chow chow (see Essentials, page 151).

Energy KJs	Protein	Total fat
332	**7g**	**2g**

Saturated fat	Carbohy-drate	Sodium
.4g	**8g**	**120mg**

Roast pork kebabs

MAKES 12

ROASTED GARLIC PASTE

1 whole bulb garlic, stalk removed
1 teaspoon vegetable oil
pinch salt
white pepper to taste

PORK KEBABS

300g pork leg, meat diced
1 teaspoon vegetable oil
pinch salt
white pepper to taste
1–2 tablespoons roasted garlic paste
1 x quantity roast vegetable kebabs
  (see page 74)

FOR THE GARLIC PASTE

1. Preheat oven to 170°C.
2. Place garlic in a roasting dish, drizzle with oil, and season with salt and pepper. Roast for 15 minutes until soft.
3. Remove from oven, leaving oven on. Once cool, squeeze flesh from garlic cloves into a bowl and mash.

FOR THE KEBABS

1. Increase oven temperature to 180°C.
2. Season pork with oil, salt and pepper.
3. Heat a frying pan, add pork and sear on all sides until golden. Add garlic paste and mix so the pork is coated.
4. Prepare roast vegetable kebabs following recipe on page 74 up to step 4.
5. Place pork along with roast vegetables on skewers when cool enough to handle. Place skewers in an oven dish. Roast in preheated oven for 10 minutes.

Serve with apple chow chow (see Essentials, page 151).

You don't have to save stuffing for the full Sunday roast occasions. Why not make it for just one or two people and serve with roast chicken legs rather than a whole chook? The smoked essence is not essential but it does add another layer to the flavour. You can buy it at most specialty food stores. And my plea to all those people who don't like Brussels sprouts — try this coleslaw and you'll be a convert!

Energy KJs	Protein	Total fat
1486	**27g**	**21g**

Saturated fat	Carbohy-drate	Sodium
5g	**14g**	**220mg**

Roast Stuffed Chicken leg
with tomato tarragon salsa

MAKES 6

STUFFED CHICKEN LEGS

6 skinless, boneless chicken legs

4 slices Vogel's bread, made into breadcrumbs

½ onion, diced

3 cloves roasted garlic, crushed

1 teaspoon smoke essence

2 egg whites

1 tablespoon chopped fresh sage

½ tablespoon each chopped fresh rosemary and thyme

zest of ¼ lemon

1 teaspoon oil

1 tablespoon chopped fresh sage

½ tablespoon each chopped fresh rosemary and thyme

pinch salt and white pepper to taste

TOMATO TARRAGON SALSA

3 large tomatoes, deseeded and diced

2 tablespoons chopped fresh tarragon

3 tablespoons finely chopped shallots

4 tablespoons olive oil

FOR THE CHICKEN

1. Preheat oven to 180°C.
2. Butterfly thigh meat by cutting each leg in half and opening it out like a book.
3. Mix together breadcrumbs, onion, garlic, smoke essence, egg whites and first measures of sage, rosemary and thyme.
4. In a separate bowl mix lemon zest and oil with second measures of herbs. Lightly season with salt and white pepper.
5. Place 2 tablespoons of breadcrumb stuffing in the middle of each butterflied chicken thigh. Fold thigh meat over stuffing.
6. Rub lemon zest and herb mixture over the outside of each chicken leg and secure with butcher's netting.
7. Heat an ovenproof frying pan to low and lightly brown both sides of chicken legs.
8. Place in preheated oven for 15 minutes, making sure the juices run clear before removing from oven. Remove netting to serve.

FOR THE SALSA

1. Mix all ingredients together and add a pinch of salt and white pepper to taste.

Serve chicken with tomato tarragon salsa, bean and Brussels slaw (see Essentials, page 158) and roast vegetable kebabs (see page 74).

Marinating the brisket overnight enables you to cook what is traditionally a tough meat really quickly without overcooking it. Don't let it cook through and dry out, serve this one medium. This is also a great addition to the barbecue. (The raisin chutney I made for the mussel burger would go down a treat with this one too!)

Energy KJs **1864**	Protein **34g**	Total fat **15g**
Saturated fat **3g**	Carbohydrate **42g**	Sodium **690mg**

Beef sandwich

SERVES 6

DAY 1

1kg beef brisket, trimmed
juice of 4 lemons
½ teaspoon sea salt
1 teaspoon cracked pepper
1 tablespoon oil

DAY 2

1 tablespoon chopped fresh
 rosemary
1 tablespoon chopped fresh thyme
2 cloves garlic, crushed
1 tablespoon crushed pepper
pinch salt

TO ASSEMBLE

6 wholemeal buns
6 tablespoons Brussels slaw (see
 Essentials, page 158)
6 tablespoons chow chow (see
 Essentials, page 151)

DAY 1

1. Score both sides of beef at a 45 degree angle against the grain of the meat, slicing about a quarter of the way through the meat.
2. Mix lemon juice, salt, pepper and oil together and rub over meat.
3. Place meat in a plastic bag. Remove the air from the bag, secure and leave in refrigerator overnight.

DAY 2

1. Preheat oven to 200°C.
2. Remove meat from marinade.
3. Mix rosemary, thyme, garlic, pepper and salt together. Rub all over meat.
4. Heat a heavy-based frying pan until hot. Sear brisket on both sides until brown. Place in preheated oven and cook for 5 minutes.
5. Remove from oven, place meat on a rack over a tray, cover with aluminium foil and rest for 10 minutes.

TO ASSEMBLE

Slice brisket into six pieces. Serve in a wholemeal bun with Brussels slaw and chow chow.

These weren't a huge hit and yes, most people went for the American hot dog cart next door, but the people who did try my green sausages loved them! I've pulled back a bit on the amount of greens so they don't look so freaky, but if you want to, go ahead and throw in some spinach and give the kids a fright!

Energy KJs	Protein	Total fat
1213	**33g**	**9g**

Saturated fat	Carbohydrate	Sodium
3g	**20g**	**634mg**

Chicken sausage spirals
with tomato and apple sauce

SERVES 4

CHICKEN SAUSAGE SPIRALS

500g chicken mince

100g lean bacon, chopped

1 spring onion, diced

¼ leek, diced

2 cloves garlic, crushed

½ teaspoon white pepper

½ teaspoon black pepper

50g fresh breadcrumbs

sausage casing

TOMATO AND APPLE SAUCE

3 tomatoes, halved

2 apples, peeled, cored and quartered

2 sprigs rosemary, 10cm long

2 cloves garlic, peeled and smashed

1 teaspoon thyme leaves

pinch salt

freshly ground black pepper to taste

½ teaspoon olive oil

FOR THE CHICKEN SAUSAGE SPIRALS

1. Place chicken, bacon, spring onion, leek, garlic, white and black pepper and breadcrumbs in a food processor or blender, and process to combine. The mixture should be soft.

2. Fill sausage skins with chicken mixture to make 4 long, skinny sausages. Roll each into a spiral lollypop and insert a skewer through the centre to hold it together.

3. Spray a heavy-based frying pan with a little oil. Pan-fry spirals over a low heat until cooked, approximately 10–15 minutes.

FOR THE TOMATO AND APPLE SAUCE

1. Preheat oven to 180°C.

2. Place tomatoes and apples on a baking tray. Sprinkle over rosemary, garlic, thyme and salt and pepper. Roast for 30 minutes.

3. Remove tomato skins and discard rosemary, thyme and garlic. Place tomatoes and apples in a blender and blend until smooth.

4. Place sauce in a saucepan and simmer to reduce by half.

5. Transfer to a jar or jug, add olive oil and store in refrigerator until needed.

I love my chilli chicken hot but you can easily adjust the chilli levels to suit your tolerance for heat. Panko crumbs give this a really crisp bite.

Energy KJs	Protein	Total fat
1428	**38g**	**8g**

Saturated fat	Carbohydrate	Sodium
3g	**28g**	**319mg**

my Chilli Chicken

SERVES 4

CHILLI MIXTURE

1 teaspoon chilli powder
1 teaspoon paprika
1 teaspoon smoked paprika
pinch salt

CHICKEN

2 cups panko crumbs
3 egg whites, beaten
1 tablespoon water
2 skinless, boneless chicken breasts,
   cut in half lengthwise
2 skinless chicken legs, cut into
   thigh and drumstick

FOR THE CHILLI MIXTURE

1. Mix all ingredients together.

FOR THE CHICKEN

1. Preheat oven to 165°C. Line a baking tray with baking paper.
2. Place panko crumbs in a bowl and add chilli mixture.
3. Whisk egg whites and water together in a bowl.
4. Dip chicken pieces in egg white mixture, then roll chicken in panko crumbs and chilli mixture. Place on prepared baking tray.
5. Bake for 30–40 minutes.

For an authentic fast-food chicken meal, serve with citrus mash (see Essentials, page 156), coleslaw (see Essentials, page 158) and lemonade (see Essentials, page 163).

This is the Food Truck's take on southern-fried chicken (and another famous chicken), which tastes great but is also just full of fat. This is baked in the oven rather than being deep-fried and you will love the flavour and crispness.

Energy KJs	Protein	Total fat
1407	**31g**	**9g**

Saturated fat	Carbohydrate	Sodium
3g	**41g**	**260mg**

my 13-herbs-and-spices chicken

SERVES 4

MY 13 HERBS AND SPICES

1 teaspoon vegetable oil
½ teaspoon dried oregano
½ teaspoon dried parsley
½ teaspoon dried sage
½ teaspoon dried thyme
½ teaspoon mustard powder
½ teaspoon turmeric
½ teaspoon white pepper
½ teaspoon coarsely ground black
   pepper
pinch salt
½ teaspoon smoked paprika
½ teaspoon ground ginger
½ teaspoon garlic powder
pinch chicken stock powder

CHICKEN

1 cup potato flour
1 cup cornflour
3 egg whites, beaten
1 tablespoon water
2 skinless, boneless chicken breasts,
   cut in half lengthwise
2 skinless chicken legs, cut into
   thigh and drumstick

FOR THE HERBS AND SPICES

1. Heat oil in a heavy-based frying pan, add oregano, parsley, sage and thyme and fry until crisp. Drain and cool herbs. When cool, grind in a mortar and pestle.
2. Place herbs in a bowl and add remaining ingredients.

FOR THE CHICKEN

1. Preheat oven to 165°C. Line a baking tray with baking paper.
2. Place potato flour and cornflour in a bowl.
3. Whisk egg whites and water together.
4. Dip chicken pieces in egg white mixture, then roll in flour and then spice mixture. Place on baking tray.
5. Bake for 30–40 minutes.

Serve with citrus mash (see Essentials, page 156), coleslaw (see Essentials, page 158) and lemonade (see Essentials, page 163).

RIGHT: *Food trucks are suddenly trendy, but they are hardly new in New Zealand. The pie carts that used to be found all round the country are the original purveyors of fast food on wheels. This photo shows Auckland's White Lady, pictured in 1960.*

A brief history of
Fast Food in New Zealand

BY ANDRÉ TABER

In early winter 1883, a hungry Mr PW Barlow wandered up Auckland's Hobson Street. He had just emigrated from England with his wife, six children and a servant girl, and he was keen to find somewhere to eat in his new town. He was about to discover New Zealand's original fast food, and several years later wrote about his experience:

I espied to my great joy a small shop with a blaze of light in the window, above which shone forth the legend 'Oyster Saloon'. I beheld a neatly dressed and pretty young lady standing behind a little counter, and apparently fully occupied in doing nothing. On the counter stood some pickle bottles filled with extremely unpleasing-looking objects resembling large white slugs, while a heap of oysters with curiously corrugated shells were piled in one corner.

Entering the establishment, I requested to be informed of the price of oysters. 'A bob a bottle! Oysters ain't sold here by the dozen; they are sold by the bottle! There are about four or five dozen, I reckon, in one of these!'

'But are those really good to eat?' I stammered. 'Try them,' she replied, spooning from a bottle about a dozen on a plate, and pushing it, together with a fork and a pepper-box, before me.

In a remarkably short space of time the plate was emptied. 'Capital! By Jove! I could not have believed they would be so good! How do you keep them fresh?' 'Oh, the boys pick them fresh for us every day, and what are not sold are thrown away.'

Mr Barlow had some more and then bought a bottle to take back to his family.

The only thing that surprises historians of food in New Zealand about this account is that during his half-hour visit to the oyster saloon, Mr Barlow appeared to be the only customer. That's because in colonial New Zealand there was high demand for fast, cheap meals, created by a population on the move — either as new immigrants or around the country in search of opportunities. They lived in boarding houses or other rented accommodation without cooking facilities. Most were single and most male.

One thing that seems to have been absent from the New Zealand landscape at the time was hawkers selling cheap ready-to-eat snacks, common in most large cities around the world. But restaurants have peppered New Zealand towns since settlers started arriving. Those restaurants served soups, chops, pies, sandwiches, ham, roasts, cheese, puddings, ale, wine and coffee. While this isn't 'fast food' as we know it today, a quick meal eaten at a counter or a small restaurant table was the historical equivalent.

Oyster saloons like the one Mr Barlow visited often also sold grilled fish. In Britain at around the same time, fried fish and chips were starting to be sold, and the meal arrived here pretty soon afterwards, remaining a favourite ever since. Advances in transportation, refrigeration and cooking technology meant that fish and chip shops could open up in areas far from the sea.

The earliest evidence in newspaper archives of fish and potato chips being sold together here is from 1900, when George Simpkin's Silver Grid restaurant in Palmerston North advertised its specialities as 'grilled potato chips, fish fried in oils, and curries'. And even though Mr Simpkin didn't say that his meals were available to take home, plenty of other fish and chip shops from that era did. It's interesting that curry may very well also have been an early takeaway option, though the curries at the Silver Grid would have been the colonial version — with generic curry powder dumped into a meat stew at the end of cooking. (Though even today many foodies will argue that Indian takeaways swimming in cream-and-tomato-paste sauce are nothing like the food you get in India.)

We don't know how many takeaway shops there were in New Zealand, but we do know that takeaways were an important part of the nation's eating habits throughout the twentieth century: people of all ages have fond memories of going down to the fish shop to collect Friday dinner. Once sales figures were being gathered, they showed it wasn't until the mid-1990s that the amount of money New Zealanders spent on restaurant meals overtook that spent on takeaways.

Historians can chart the history of fast food through advertisements in newspapers, but unfortunately people didn't write much about everyday meals like a pie or fish and chips, bought from down the road and scoffed straight from the wrapping. Consequently we know very little about what the interior of the shops looked and smelled like, what recipes were used and, most importantly, what the food tasted like. Food historian Tony Simpson once found a curious mention of the batter on fried fish being used just as a cooking medium, which was then discarded and only the fish eaten.

Meat pies in the past were plain. In 1904, the grandfather of third-generation Hokitika baker Bernard Preston served giblet pie to Prime Minister Dick Seddon; a baking book from the 1930s contains the recipe for the Prestons' meat-pie filling: boil beef and potatoes and season with salt and pepper. The starch from the potatoes would have made a satisfyingly silky gravy, and the flavour would have been very meaty. Cheese wasn't added to meat pies until the 1970s.

Roast meats were a popular option for quick meals in the nineteenth century: given the basic oven technology available at the time, roasting was the most effective way to cook meat, and a joint could be prepared in advance of meal service, along with spuds, and served almost instantaneously when the customer ordered. Cold roast meat would be used as a sandwich

LEFT: *A 1965 photo of the famous Frisco burger bar, located in an old hotel on the corner of Great South and Manukau roads in Auckland. There's a car sales yard on the site these days.*

filling. This style of meal survives: most New Zealanders live within driving distance of a takeaway roast shop.

If you're in Arrowtown you can see the remains of what might have been the first Chinese restaurant in New Zealand. Su Sing's long house was built around 1870, and served as a store and restaurant for the community of Chinese miners. There were other Chinese eating houses built in the Otago goldfields at the time, and when the goldmining ended some of this community drifted to North Island towns, where they also established restaurants.

From time to time European New Zealanders decided to check out these establishments. In 1887 the *Tuapeka Times* called Chinese restaurants, with their dainty teapots, chopsticks, soy sauce, tender meats and expertly prepared rice, 'a novelty to the most blasé gourmet'.

In the first half of the twentieth century, six o'clock closing underpinned the demand for quick meals and takeaways. Bars no longer served food and restaurants were not allowed to serve alcohol, which meant that out of necessity restaurants targeted what we would today call the 'casual' end of the market. Tea rooms, more aimed at women, also served this function. Bacon and eggs, steak and eggs, or steak and chips took over as the food of choice.

Horse-drawn pie carts appeared on city streets at the turn of the twentieth century (and judging by court reports were already known as the place to look for a late-night fight), but by the time they became iconic fast-food establishments in the 1950s they were,

ironically, dropping pies from the menu in favour of hamburgers. Daytime snacks of cakes and pastries were available in places like tea rooms.

American influences on New Zealand fast food go back all the way to oyster saloons, which originated in New York. Coca-Cola was being served in cafés by World War I, and health food was popularised by Kellogg's and their ready-made breakfast cereals. The 1930s saw an explosion of health-food and vegetarian cafés — the Sanitarium company (started by followers of Dr John Harvey Kellogg) ran a chain which served vegetarian soups, omelettes and nutmeat. Milk bars, with their ice-cream sundaes and milk shakes, were well established by the mid-1930s, but wouldn't start serving hamburgers until World War II, when 100,000 American servicemen passed through New Zealand.

In the 1950s there was an increase in Chinese immigration, and the restaurants this community subsequently opened became much more popular with the general population. Migrants from Greece, the Balkans, Italy and the Netherlands also found food service a good way to get into business in New Zealand. However, they all knew Anglo food was what their customers wanted — hence the Chinese takeaway that serves burgers and fish and chips alongside chow mein and fried rice.

In 1971 a much less subtle invasion of New Zealand's stomachs began with the arrival of Kentucky Fried Chicken in Auckland's Royal Oak, serving traditional southern-style battered and deep-fried chicken. It was so popular that within two years it was reported to be using

15 per cent of the country's total chicken production. KFC also very quickly acquired local competitors: Big Rooster and Homestead Chicken. These fast-food purveyors based their operations on production-line speed and consistency, cheap youth workers, franchised ownership and an image of spotless cleanliness. The most celebrated of these companies, McDonald's, was beaten to New Zealand by three years by Wimpy, which opened its first burger bar in 1973. Wimpy was a chain which had been run by the Lyons catering empire in the UK since 1954, using the same American fast-food business principles. Georgie Pie, a New Zealand company selling overtly Kiwi food in an Americanised fast-food setting, operated from 1977 to 1998.

Italian food has been on the menu for New Zealanders for a long time. Macaroni and spaghetti were available in the 1800s, and were sometimes prepared with tomato-based sauces. With the 'continental-style' restaurant boom of the 1960s (and, once again, with no small amount of influence from America), pasta became an acceptable eating-out dish. Takeaway pizza was certainly available by the early 1970s, and when Pizza Hut opened in New Lynn, Auckland, in 1974, people were already at loggerheads about whether thin or thick crusts were the most authentic.

The 'big three' American franchises — McDonald's, KFC and Pizza Hut — started in the 1950s as take-outs, but by the 1970s they had embraced eat-in, and their first New Zealand establishments were promoted as family restaurants. Despite this, the media understood that their arrival signalled the end of 'traditional' takeaways. Their predictions came to fruition in the 1990s when, with an increasing appetite for international cuisines (which didn't happen in New Zealand alone — even in places as diverse as France and Japan there were fashions for 'foreign' food) and a more cosmopolitan mix of immigrants who opened restaurants, our takeaway mix suddenly included Mexican, Thai, Vietnamese, Turkish, Indian, sushi, bagels, panini and so on. But history seems to have come full circle, with food courts and cafés catering to a new demand for quick sit-down meals.

But wait, not so fast . . . It turns out fish and chips hung in there for a lot longer than people expected. In 2003, a Nielsen survey showed that fish and chips were clearly still the favourite fast food of New Zealanders. They asked interviewees what fast food they had eaten in the last month and 55 per cent had eaten fish and chips. McDonald's was at 40 per cent, KFC 29 per cent, Chinese 28 per cent, Burger King 17 per cent and Pizza Hut 14 per cent. In 2005, the company DigiPoll asked people about their most common choice of takeaway, and 32 per cent chose 'Asian food', 29 per cent fish and chips, 11 per cent pizza, 9 per cent hamburgers, and 6 per cent KFC. Pies didn't make any of those lists, but symbolically, flavours from just about every world cuisine are available encased in flaky pastry and called, enthusiastically, a Kiwi pie.

SOURCES

PW Barlow, *Kaipara; Or, Experiences of a Settler in North New Zealand*, Southern Reprints, 1993.

Ian Brailsford, 'US Image But NZ Venture: Americana and Fast-Food Advertising in New Zealand, 1971–1990', in *Australasian Journal of American Studies*, December 2003.

Harvey Levenstein, *Paradox of Plenty: A Social History of Eating in Modern America*, Oxford University Press, 1993.

Papers Past, New Zealand digitised newspapers and periodicals, www.paperspast.natlib.govt.nz

Perrin Rowland, *Dining Out: A History of the Restaurant in New Zealand*, Auckland University Press, 2010.

Restaurant Association of New Zealand, *2003 Pocket Factbook*, *2008 Foodservice Facts*.

Te Ara: The Encyclopedia of New Zealand, www.teara.govt.nz

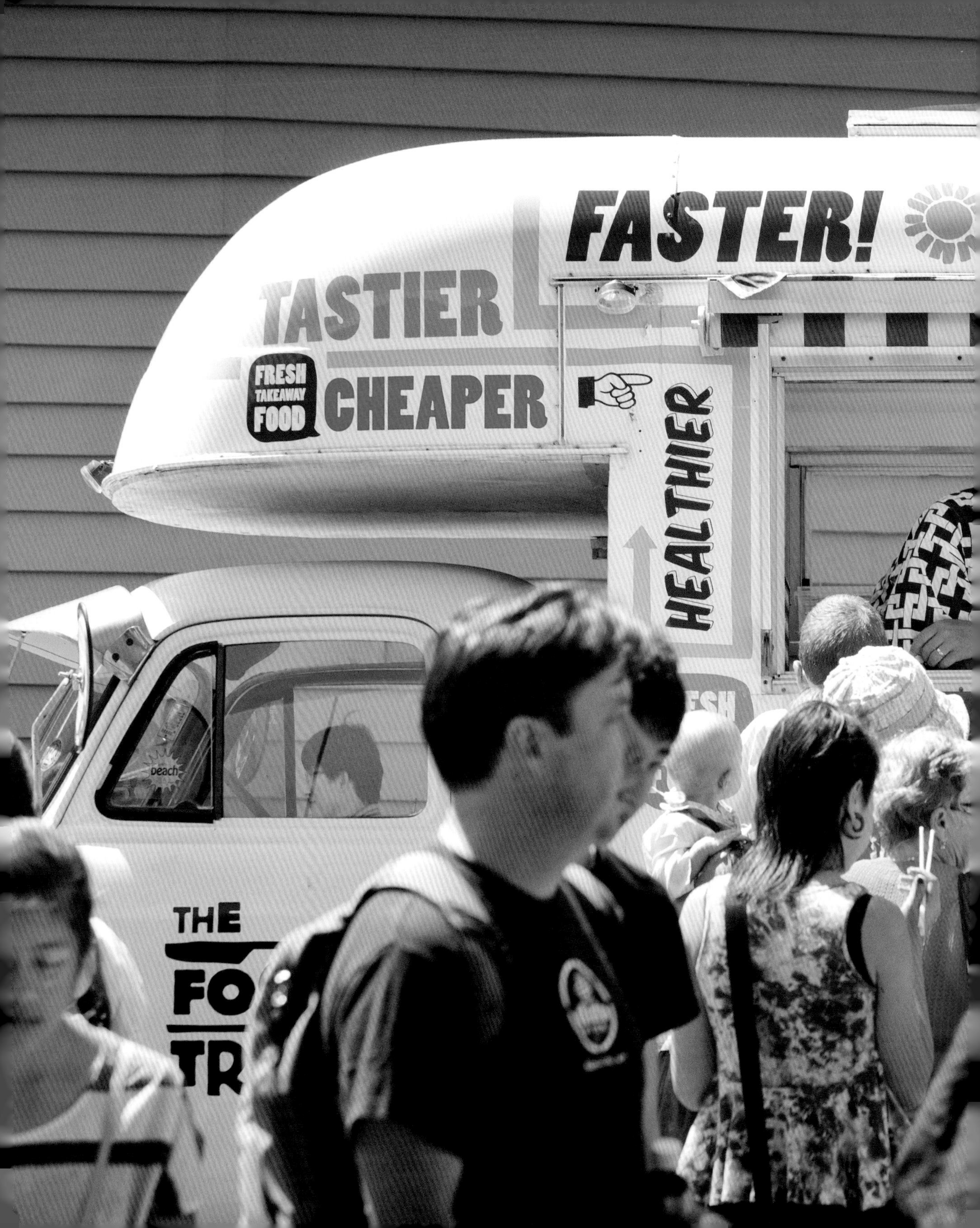
FASTER!
TASTIER
FRESH TAKEAWAY FOOD
CHEAPER
HEALTHIER

TASTIER

FRESH TAKEAWAY FOOD HEALTHIER

TASTIER

The Great OE

Chinese, Indian, Mexican and Japanese

This is quite a fancy dish, one of the fanciest the Food Truck kitchen has turned out. It's so good you could easily serve it at the start of a dinner party. Disappointingly, we only sold about three of these at the Chinese New Year Festival, but the next week I put them on the menu at Molten and they sold like hot cakes!

Energy KJs	Protein	Total fat
1953	**20g**	**20g**

Saturated fat	Carbohydrate	Sodium
4g	**46g**	**632mg**

Chicken and tofu dumplings
with miso-roasted eggplant, crispy leeks and master stock

SERVES 4

MASTER STOCK
Makes about 1 litre

1 knob ginger, golf-ball sized

1 stalk lemon grass

1 onion, peeled and quartered

1 red chilli, halved and deseeded

1 tablespoon coriander stalks and leaves

1 tablespoon black peppercorns

3 bay leaves

1 litre water

1 tablespoon low-sodium soy sauce

3 tablespoons brown sugar

2 cloves garlic, peeled

4 tablespoons Chinese sherry

DUMPLING PASTRY
Makes 12

125g flour

pinch salt

1 egg

2 egg yolks

1 tablespoon olive oil

FOR THE STOCK

1. Place all ingredients in a large saucepan. Bring to the boil, then reduce heat and simmer for 5 minutes.
2. Strain into a jug and store in refrigerator until required.

FOR THE DUMPLING PASTRY

1. Place flour and salt in a food processor. Add egg and process. Then add egg yolks and oil and process until a dough forms. Add more flour or water if necessary.
2. Roll dough out to 2.5mm thickness. Cut into 12 circles the size of a saucer.

Recipe continued over page…

Chicken and tofu dumplings continued…

DUMPLING FILLING

1 teaspoon olive oil
½ cup shiitake or oyster mushrooms
250g chicken mince
1 tablespoon milk
1 egg
100g soft tofu
pinch salt
pinch white pepper
2 tablespoons chopped chives

MISO-ROASTED EGGPLANT

2 eggplant, cut in half lengthwise
   and flesh scored into diamonds
1 tablespoon yellow miso paste
2 tablespoons olive oil

CRISPY LEEKS

½ leek, white part only, washed
   and sliced lengthwise into 4cm
   matchsticks
1 tablespoon cornflour
canola oil for frying
pinch salt

WOK-FRIED ASIAN GREENS

2 pak choy, washed and sliced into
   quarters
2 bok choy, washed and sliced into
   quarters
1 teaspoon water

FOR THE DUMPLINGS

1. Heat olive oil in a frying pan until just smoking. Add mushrooms and stir-fry for 30 seconds. Drain on paper towels, cool and then slice.
2. Place chicken in a food processor and process until smooth. Add milk, egg and tofu and process to combine well. Transfer mixture to a bowl. Season with salt and pepper and add chives. Mix together.
3. Spoon 1 tablespoon of filling into the centre of each dumpling wrapper. Moisten edges with water and fold over to make a half circle. Press edges together. Curl into a crescent around your finger and join edges to form tortellini.
4. Bring a large saucepan of water to the boil. Add dumplings and boil for 10 minutes. They will float to the top when cooked. Drain.

FOR THE EGGPLANT

1. Preheat oven to 180°C.
2. Mix together miso and olive oil and spoon over scored eggplant. Place in a baking dish.
3. Bake for 20–25 minutes.
4. Remove from oven and cool. Scoop out flesh, mash and place on a plate.

FOR THE LEEKS

1. Toss leeks in cornflour.
2. Heat oil in a saucepan to 160°C.
3. Add leeks and cook until golden. Drain on paper towels and season with salt.

FOR THE GREENS

1. Heat a wok or frying pan and spray with a little olive oil.
2. Add pak choy, bok choy and water and stir-fry for 30 seconds.

Serve chicken and tofu dumplings on miso-roasted eggplant. Top with wok-fried Asian greens, pour over master stock and scatter with crispy leeks and microgreens.

HEALTHIER TASTIER FASTER!

HEALTHIER FAST TASTI

FOOD

HEAPER
'ALTHIER

FRESH
TAKEAWAY
FOOD

HEALTHIER FASTER! TASTIER

FASTER!
HEALTHIER

✳ HEALTHIER ✳

A really simple, fast, tasty way to eat noodles. It's colourful and vibrant, and can be piled into a noodle box and taken to eat out-of-doors. After you've tried it you will never look at two-minute noodles again!

Energy KJs	Protein	Total fat
2715	**40g**	**40g**

Saturated fat	Carbohydrate	Sodium
6g	**30g**	**741mg**

Noodles with squid
and citrus dressing

SERVES 4

SQUID

1 teaspoon low-sodium soy sauce

2 cloves garlic, crushed

1 teaspoon chilli powder

1 teaspoon olive oil

2 teaspoons brown sugar

4 tubes squid, cleaned and cut open

CORIANDER PESTO

1 bunch coriander, finely chopped

10 mint leaves, finely chopped

4 tablespoons chopped toasted walnuts

pinch salt

freshly ground black pepper to taste

4 tablespoons olive oil

CITRUS DRESSING

1 cup grapefruit juice

1 tablespoon mandarin juice

1 tablespoon lemon juice

1 egg yolk

pinch salt

pinch sugar

4 tablespoons olive oil

FOR THE SQUID

1. Mix soy sauce, garlic, chilli powder, olive oil and brown sugar together and spread over squid. Place in a dish, cover and refrigerate for 1 hour.
2. Heat a barbecue plate or heavy-based frying pan to very hot. Sear squid tubes for about 30 seconds on each side.
3. Remove from heat. Cool and slice thinly.

FOR THE PESTO

1. Mix together all ingredients and set aside.

FOR THE DRESSING

1. Place grapefruit, mandarin and lemon juices in a saucepan. Bring to the boil, lower heat and simmer until reduced to 4 tablespoons. Remove from heat and cool.
2. Place cooled juices, egg yolk, salt, sugar and olive oil in a screw-top jar and shake to combine.

Recipe continued over page…

Noodles with squid and citrus dressing continued...

NOODLES

500g egg noodles

1 telegraph cucumber, peeled, deseeded and sliced lengthwise into ribbons

2 carrots, peeled and sliced into ribbons

2 spring onions, finely sliced

FOR THE NOODLES

1. Cook noodles according to packet instructions.

Combine cooked noodles, dressing, cucumber, carrots and spring onions. Add sliced squid and toss to mix. Divide among plates and garnish with coriander pesto.

We all know that sweet and sour is so good but also so bad for you. Here's a recipe that exactly reflects what the Food Truck is all about: recreating great takeaway food, at home, the healthy way.

Energy KJs	Protein	Total fat
1086	**28g**	**7g**

Saturated fat	Carbohydrate	Sodium
2g	**20g**	**448mg**

Pork Chopsticks
with sweet and sour sauce

SERVES 4

PORK CHOPSTICKS

500g lean pork shoulder, cut into 2cm cubes

1 tablespoon grated fresh ginger

1 tablespoon olive oil

pinch salt

SWEET AND SOUR SAUCE

1 x 400g can whole peeled tomatoes

4 tablespoons red wine vinegar

4 tablespoons honey

1 knob ginger, walnut sized

2 cloves garlic

1–2 tablespoons cornflour

½ x 325g can pineapple chunks in juice

2 red capsicum, deseeded and sliced

2 rice crackers, crushed, to garnish

microgreens, to garnish

FOR THE PORK

1. Thread pork cubes onto 4 chopsticks. Mix together ginger, oil and salt and brush over pork. Place in a dish, cover and leave overnight.
2. Preheat oven to 180°C.
3. Heat a heavy-based frying pan. Add pork and brown on all sides.
4. Bake in oven for 5 minutes.

FOR THE SAUCE

1. Place tomatoes, vinegar, honey, ginger and garlic in a saucepan. Bring to the boil and simmer for 3 minutes.
2. Remove ginger and garlic. Mix cornflour with a little water and add to pan to thicken sauce, then stir in pineapple and capsicum.

Place pork chopsticks on plates and drizzle with sweet and sour sauce. Sprinkle with crushed rice crackers and microgreens.

Ching of the Canton Café

This Kingsland restaurant is one of the most popular in Auckland. There's always a queue outside the door and inside it's fast and furious. The moment you finish eating there's another group of people wanting to grab the table from you. It's easy to see why so many people want to eat here. The food is great. Ching told me that he cooks nothing ahead. All his ingredients are carefully prepped and he uses them as he needs them. He cooks everything as quickly as possible and I was surprised by how little soy, sugar and salt he used. He allows all the natural flavours to come through and the result is just awesome.

These are really punchy, really flavoursome treats inspired by Jose's tacos from Mexican Specialities. And they are fun to make. You could serve them as a starter for a dinner with friends or as a weekend lunch dish. If you don't have or want to use prawns, use any other sort of fish, in the same marinade. You could even go the full hog and make your own tacos using masa flour — it's even easier if you have a tortilla press.

Energy KJs	Protein	Total fat
1736	**20g**	**12g**

Saturated fat	Carbohydrate	Sodium
2g	**55g**	**455mg**

SOFT TACOS
with marinated prawns and beans with lime dressing

SERVES 4

MARINATED PRAWNS
32 prawns, peeled and deveined
½ onion, finely sliced
¼ teaspoon smoked chilli powder
   or smoked paprika
½ teaspoon olive oil
pinch salt

BEANS WITH LIME DRESSING
juice of 2 limes
1 tablespoon honey
2 tablespoons olive oil
pinch salt
24 French or long beans, cut in half
   and blanched

TACOS
8 small soft tortillas
½ cup El Speciale Sauce (see
   Essentials, page 152)
cos lettuce leaves

FOR THE PRAWNS
1. Place all ingredients in a bowl and toss gently. Cover and place in refrigerator for about 15 minutes.
2. Just before you're ready to serve the tacos, cook prawns. Heat a heavy-based frying pan, add prawns and cook until charred on both sides.

FOR THE BEANS
1. Mix all ingredients together and set aside.

FOR THE TACOS
1. Warm tortillas according to packet instructions
2. Place 4 prawns on each tortilla with 1 tablespoon of El Speciale Sauce, a few cos leaves and 1–2 tablespoons of beans. Fold and serve.

If desired, sprinkle with microgreens and a squeeze of lime juice.

I first saw this dish being made in Mexico when I went on an NZTE trip. In Mexico City, restaurants called barbacao — Spanish for barbecue — serve a special sort of slow-cooked lamb on Sundays only.

Energy KJs	Protein	Total fat
3262	**47g**	**33g**

Saturated fat	Carbohydrate	Sodium
6g	**74g**	**563mg**

corn tostada
with shredded lamb

SERVES 4

TOSTADA

5 fresh corn cobs
juice of 1 lime
pinch salt
½ cup flax seeds

SHREDDED LAMB

1 x 400g lamb shoulder, bone out
1 teaspoon chopped fresh chilli
pinch salt
white pepper to taste
1 clove garlic, crushed
1 teaspoon olive oil
1 teaspoon smoked paprika
1 x 390g can corn kernels, drained
1 x 390g can black beans, drained
2 tablespoons chopped coriander

TO ASSEMBLE

2 tablespoons El Speciale Sauce (see Essentials, page 152)
coriander sprigs to garnish

FOR THE TOSTADA

1. Preheat oven to 120°C.
2. Remove kernels from corn cobs. Place in a food processor and process. Transfer corn mixture to a bowl and add lime juice, salt and flax seeds. Mix to form a batter.
3. Spread mixture evenly over silicone baking sheets to a thickness of 3–4mm.
4. Place in preheated oven and leave overnight.
5. Increase oven temperature to 180°C. Cut cooked corn mixture into 8 circles about the size of a saucer.
6. Toast in preheated oven for 3–4 minutes or until golden brown.

FOR THE LAMB

1. Place lamb in a baking dish. Grind chilli, salt, pepper, garlic, olive oil and smoked paprika together in a mortar and pestle to form a paste. Spread on lamb and marinate for 1 hour.
2. Preheat oven to 150°C.
3. Heat a heavy-based frying pan. Place lamb in pan and brown on all sides. Remove and wrap in aluminium foil. Place in a roasting dish.
4. Roast for 2 hours.
5. Remove lamb from oven and cool. When cool enough to handle, shred and place in a bowl along with corn, black beans and coriander.

Spread each tostada with El Speciale Sauce and top with shredded lamb mixture. Garnish with sprigs of coriander.

Jose of Mexican Specialities

Jose really opened my eyes to the subtlety of authentic Mexican food. It's been really Americanised over the years, and all that sour cream and artificially flavoured corn chips are miles away from the fresh, clean flavours that great, simply prepared Mexican food has in spades.

This is my take on the classic saagwalla. By using thinly sliced lamb backstrap you can make a curry really quickly so there's no mucking about. Fresh spinach gives it great colour and nutrition.

Energy KJs	Protein	Total fat
633	**15g**	**6g**

Saturated fat	Carbohydrate	Sodium
1.6g	**9.6g**	**218mg**

Lamb Curry

SERVES 6

LAMB

3 lamb backstraps, thinly sliced

1 teaspoon Food Truck garam masala (see Essentials, page 162)

1 teaspoon vegetable oil

CURRY PASTE

2 onions, chopped

1 bunch coriander, stalks only

4 cloves garlic, crushed

3 tablespoons Food Truck garam masala

½ cup water

pinch salt

white pepper to taste

CURRY SAUCE

1 clove garlic, chopped

1 teaspoon chopped ginger

2 shallots, chopped

2 tablespoons Food Truck garam masala

1 teaspoon vegetable oil

8 okra, sliced

1 green capsicum, deseeded and diced

2 tomatoes, chopped

4 tindori or 1 Lebanese cucumber, chopped

1 cup water

1 sprig curry leaf

1 bunch spinach, blanched, pressed and chopped

1 bunch coriander leaves

1 teaspoon chopped mint

FOR THE LAMB

1. Toss lamb in garam masala and oil.
2. Heat a heavy-based pan to hot. Stir-fry lamb until brown. Set aside.

FOR THE PASTE

1. Blend onions, coriander stalks, garlic, garam masala and water together in a blender. Place in a saucepan and bring to the boil. Reduce heat and simmer for approximately 10 minutes until thick. Season with salt and white pepper to taste.

FOR THE CURRY SAUCE

1. Stir garlic, ginger, shallots, garam masala, oil, okra, green capsicum, tomatoes and tindori in to the curry paste. Add water and then curry leaf sprig. Continue cooking until mixture is reduced and thick. Add lamb, then spinach, coriander leaves and mint. Remove curry leaf sprig before serving.

Here I've used eggplant as my major ingredient, but this curry can take just about any vegetable you've got lurking around in the bottom of your fridge. It really is the fridge-cleaner curry!

Energy KJs	Protein	Total fat
705	**7.5g**	**12g**

Saturated fat	Carbohydrate	Sodium
4g	**11g**	**147mg**

Eggplant curry

SERVES 6

3 medium eggplants, sliced lengthwise into 8 wedges

1 teaspoon olive oil

pinch salt

white pepper to taste

1 x quantity curry sauce (see page 112)

1. Preheat oven to 180°C.
2. Toss eggplant in olive oil, and salt and pepper. Place in a hot frying pan and cook until brown on both sides. Place in preheated oven and cook for 6 minutes until tender. Set aside.
3. Prepare curry sauce following recipe on page 112. Add eggplant instead of lamb to sauce. Remove curry leaf sprig before serving.

This is my take on New Zealand's most popular curry. I found most butter chicken curries were just too sweet and lacking in spice or flavour. This one uses yoghurt and coconut cream to give you that rich flavour without all the calories. If you want to be adventurous, try replacing the chicken with turkey or even rabbit!

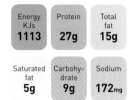

Energy KJs	Protein	Total fat
1113	**27g**	**15g**

Saturated fat	Carbohy-drate	Sodium
5g	**9g**	**172mg**

mike's 'butter' Chicken

SERVES 6

CHICKEN

6 boneless chicken thighs, sliced into strips

3 tablespoons tomato purée

1 teaspoon mild chilli powder

4 tablespoons plain low-fat yoghurt

CURRY SAUCE

1 teaspoon vegetable oil

1 teaspoon chopped ginger

1 clove garlic, chopped

2 shallots, chopped

3 tablespoons Food Truck curry powder (see page 162)

3 tomatoes, chopped

1 cup diced, peeled peaches

400ml lite coconut cream

1 cup plain low-fat yoghurt

3 tablespoons almond butter

FOR THE CHICKEN

1. Mix chicken, tomato purée, chilli powder and yoghurt together and marinate for 1 hour. Drain.
2. Heat a heavy-based frying pan, add chicken and brown on all sides. Set aside.

FOR THE SAUCE

1. Heat oil in the heavy-based frying pan, add ginger and garlic and stir-fry for 1 minute. Add shallots and cook for a further minute. Add curry powder and cook for another minute. Add tomatoes and peaches and cook for 1 minute. Add coconut cream, yoghurt and almond butter and simmer for a further 4 minutes.
2. Add cooked 'butter' chicken to sauce and reheat thoroughly.

I still can't believe how well the watermelon worked in a curry! This could be a refreshing side dish to barbecued meat, or just a great stand-alone vegetable curry. Not many people tried it in The Food Truck episode. They don't know what they missed out on!

Energy KJs	Protein	Total fat
672	**6g**	**11g**

Saturated fat	Carbohydrate	Sodium
4g	**13g**	**48mg**

watermelon curry

SERVES 6

1 x quantity curry sauce (see page 116)

FOR THE CURRY SAUCE

1. Prepare curry sauce following recipe on page 116.

WATERMELON

4 cups diced, skinless watermelon

FOR THE WATERMELON

1. Add diced watermelon to curry sauce instead of 'butter' chicken.

Bobby of Little India

Little India is a chain restaurant but with a family heart. I'll admit I was a little bit sceptical about the validity of their 'family recipes', but after meeting Bobby and the others I realised it wasn't a publicity stunt. These guys all live and breathe curries, and strictly follow grandma's recipes. Bobby taught me the importance of making my own garam masala and told me to make everything from scratch. He also told me not to use curry powder . . . so I made my own curry powder then used that!

Probably the healthiest of the dishes we made, I decided to use smoked kahawai for this because it's an iconic Kiwi ingredient and the strong, smokey flavour works really well inside sushi. The nori (seaweed) is on the inside and the seeds are on the outside, but don't let that put you off — it's just as easy as rolling normal sushi.

Energy KJs	Protein	Total fat
489	**7g**	**3g**

Saturated fat	Carbohy-drate	Sodium
.5g	**14g**	**28mg**

smoked kahawai and bean sushi

MAKES 8 PIECES

SUSHI

1 sheet nori
½ cup cooked brown sushi rice
½ cup cooked white sushi rice
1 tablespoon black sesame seeds
1 tablespoon white sesame seeds
4 shiitake mushrooms, sliced
½ cup sliced smoked kahawai
8 green beans, trimmed and
  blanched
1 long red chilli, deseeded and finely
  sliced

DRESSING

2 teaspoons sesame oil
1 teaspoon grated horseradish
½ teaspoon miso
juice of 1 lime

FOR THE SUSHI

1. Place nori sheet on a sushi mat rough side up. Spread rice firmly and evenly over nori. Spread sesame seeds over rice and pat down. Carefully, holding the nori sheet, turn over so rice is now the base layer. Press in the ends until square. Lay mushrooms, kahawai, beans and chilli in a strip in the middle. Firmly roll up nori sheet, without plastic wrap, sealing the edge with water.

FOR THE DRESSING

1. Mix all ingredients together and drizzle over sushi.

Slice roll into eight pieces and drizzle with dressing.

Why doesn't sushi just come with a salad? By adding a little side salad it not only increases your vegetable intake it also stops you from eating so many pieces of sushi. You can even use the salad as an alternative to pickled ginger or wasabi, or roll the salad inside the sushi!

Energy KJs	Protein	Total fat
178	**1.6g**	**2.8g**

Saturated fat	Carbohydrate	Sodium
.4g	**3g**	**50mg**

Salad for sushi

SALAD
¼ cucumber, finely sliced with a vegetable peeler

¼ packet snow pea sprouts, trimmed

4 beans, trimmed, blanched and sliced in half lengthwise

4 spinach leaves, torn

SALAD DRESSING
2 teaspoons sesame oil

1 teaspoon grated horseradish

½ teaspoon miso

juice of 1 lime

FOR THE SALAD AND DRESSING
1. Mix all salad ingredients together.
2. Mix all dressing ingredients together.
3. Dress salad just before serving.

I wanted to try something different here so I used turkey instead of chicken. If you have some leftover turkey from Christmas Day, why not turn it into some sushi? I served mine with grapefruit caviar but you can always just top it with cranberry sauce!

Energy KJs	Protein	Total fat
609	**14g**	**2g**

Saturated fat	Carbohy-drate	Sodium
.5g	**17g**	**150mg**

Turkey Katsu Sushi

MAKES 24 PIECES

TURKEY KATSU

2 egg whites

4 tablespoons water

2 cups panko breadcrumbs

pinch salt

white pepper to taste

1 small turkey breast (approximately size of 2 chicken breasts), cut into 1cm strips

SUSHI

4 sheets nori

2 cups cooked brown sushi rice

2 cups cooked white sushi rice

1 x quantity turkey katsu

1 apple, cored and sliced

¼ cup crushed tamari almonds

16 small leaves endive, torn in half

1 red grapefruit, cut into segments and diced, seeds removed

FOR THE KATSU

1. Beat egg whites and water together in a bowl.
2. Season panko breadcrumbs with salt and pepper in another bowl.
3. Dip turkey strips into egg white mixture, then into seasoned panko crumbs.
4. Heat a frying pan and add a little oil. Pan-fry strips until golden.

FOR THE SUSHI

1. Lay nori sheet on a sushi mat shiny side down. Press sushi rice firmly and evenly over rough side of sheet. Place a quarter of the filling ingredients, turkey katsu, apple, almonds and endive, in a strip in the middle and roll up. Repeat with remaining nori sheets and filling.
2. Slice each roll into eight pieces. Spoon grapefruit over the top.

I made the rice ball from a mixture of brown and white short-grain sushi rice. You don't need a sushi mat to roll it, just wrap it up in cling film. This was the biggest hit of the Japan Day game day on The Food Truck and would be a great thing to put into kids' lunchboxes.

Energy KJs **923**	Protein **20g**	Total fat **8g**
Saturated fat **3g**	Carbohydrate **16g**	Sodium **100mg**

Lamb rice ball

MAKES ENOUGH FOR APPROXIMATELY 8 BALLS

TERIYAKI LAMB

1 teaspoon low-sodium soy sauce
2 tablespoons honey
white pepper
500g lamb rump, sliced into stir-fry strips

FOR EACH LAMB BALL

1 nori sheet
½ cup cooked brown sushi rice
½ cup cooked white sushi rice
1 tablespoon chia seeds
1 tablespoon sunflower seeds
1 tablespoon flax seeds
2 tablespoons teriyaki lamb
1 tablespoon finely chopped cucumber
1 tablespoon finely chopped snow peas
1 teaspoon finely chopped mint

FOR THE TERIYAKI

1. Mix soy sauce, honey and pepper together. Add lamb and toss to coat. Cover and refrigerate for 1 hour.
2. Heat a heavy-based frying pan and add a little oil. Pan-fry lamb in batches. Cool.

FOR THE LAMB BALLS

1. Place nori sheet on plastic wrap, shiny side down. Press sushi rice firmly and evenly over rough side of sheet.
2. Mix seeds together and sprinkle over rice, patting them down.
3. Cover with plastic wrap and turn over. Remove outside layer of plastic wrap
4. Pile teriyaki lamb, cucumber, snow peas and mint in the middle of the nori sheet.
5. Pull corners of the plastic wrap together and form into a ball shape, twist the ends of the wrap together firmly.
6. Place in refrigerator for a minimum of two hours to set, and unwrap to eat.

Sweet Things

Drinks, smoothies and ice-creams

Why do we always only have fruit in our ice-blocks? I made this because I wondered whether kids would actually go for frozen vegetables on a stick. The beetroot one didn't really take off, but the sweetcorn went down a summer treat (even though it was a rainy summer's day).

Beetroot & pomegranate		
Energy KJs **423**	Protein **1.3g**	Total fat **.2g**
Saturated fat **0g**	Carbohydrate **24g**	Sodium **32mg**

Sweetcorn & grapefruit		
Energy KJs **330**	Protein **1.7g**	Total fat **.7g**
Saturated fat **.04g**	Carbohydrate **16g**	Sodium **3mg**

ice-blocks

MAKES 8

Beetroot, blackberry and pomegranate

3 medium beetroot, peeled and diced
1 cup frozen blackberries
2 cups pomegranate juice
2 teaspoons honey
seeds from 1 pomegranate

1. Prepare ice-block moulds following instructions below.
2. Cook beetroot in a saucepan of boiling water until tender.
3. Place in a bowl with blackberries, pomegranate juice and honey. Purée with a stick blender until smooth.
4. Sprinkle pomegranate seeds into the bottom of 6 prepared moulds. Pour beetroot mixture over the top. Freeze.

ICE-BLOCK MOULDS
6 lengths PVC piping about 10cm long
plastic wrap
rubber bands
aluminium foil

TO MAKE YOUR OWN ICE-BLOCK MOULDS
1. Cover top of each PVC length with two layers of plastic wrap and secure with rubber bands. Then cover plastic wrap with aluminium foil.
2. After the ice-block mixture has been added, cover base with aluminium foil and slide a chopstick through the foil and into the ice-block — the foil holds the stick in place.

Sweetcorn and grapefruit

4 corn cobs, cooked and cooled
2 tablespoons honey
1 cup grapefruit juice
pinch salt

1. Prepare ice-block moulds following instructions above.
2. Remove kernels from corn cobs with a knife. Place in a blender or food processor and process to a fine texture. Add honey, 1 tablespoon of grapefruit juice and salt and process again. Add remaining grapefruit juice and process to mix.
3. Strain then pour into prepared moulds. Freeze.

This was one of the hardest challenges. I found out that it's really difficult to make ice-cream without sugar. You need the sugar to help stop the ice-cream turning to ice. I didn't manage to remove all the sugar, but I got rid of half of it by using honey, which also gave it a lot more flavour.

Energy KJs	Protein	Total fat
2405	**8g**	**28g**

Saturated fat	Carbohy-drate	Sodium
15g	**74g**	**103mg**

ice-cream
with plum and cherry sauce

SERVES 6

ICE-CREAM

½ cup water

½ cup sugar

½ cup honey

2 vanilla pods, split

4 egg yolks

225g cream, whipped

225g natural, unsweetened yoghurt

PLUM AND CHERRY SAUCE

6 ripe plums, halved and stones removed

20 ripe cherries, pitted

½ cup water

1 tablespoon honey

FOR THE ICE-CREAM

1. Place water, sugar, honey and split vanilla pods in a saucepan and heat to 120°C. Take off the heat, run cold water on base of saucepan to cool, discard vanilla pods and set syrup aside.
2. Beat egg yolks until thick.
3. Pour syrup over egg yolks and beat until cool. Fold in whipped cream and yoghurt.
4. Pour ice-cream mixture into a snap-lock container and freeze overnight.

FOR THE PLUM AND CHERRY SAUCE

1. Place all ingredients in a heavy-based saucepan and bring to a simmer. Continue simmering until liquid has reduced.
2. Transfer sauce to a blender and purée until smooth.

Serve in home-made cones or in a bowl with one of the toppings on page 136.

Three great ways to have ice-cream at home: with a Brazil nut topping, with a beet tip (my take on the famous Jelly Tip), and dipped in sherbet.

Beet tip

Energy KJs	Protein	Total fat
3816	**14g**	**49g**

Saturated fat	Carbohydrate	Sodium
24g	**104g**	**182mg**

Cone ice-creams

Beet tip

1 ice-cream cone (see Essentials, page 163)

1 scoop ice-cream (see page 134)

1 slice beetroot, blackberry and pomegranate ice-block (see page 132)

crushed Brazil nuts or chocolate hail for sprinkling

1. For each beet tip, first place a scoop of ice-cream in a cone. Then follow with a slice of beetroot ice-block and sprinkle nuts or chocolate hail on top.

Brazil nut topping

1 cup Brazil nuts

½ cup fruit mix (golden raisins, cranberries, sultanas, currants)

4 tablespoons chopped dark chocolate

1. Preheat oven to 160°C.
2. Place Brazil nuts on a baking tray and roast in preheated oven for 10 minutes or until golden. Remove from oven and cool.
3. Using a pestle and mortar, crush Brazil nuts. Alternatively, place in a clean tea towel and smash with a rolling pin.
4. Place crushed nuts in a bowl, add fruit mix and chocolate and combine.

Sherbet topping

1 x quantity sherbet (see Essentials, page 163)

1. Sprinkle sherbet on top of ice-cream.

This was my take on L&P (Lemon and Van de Elzen, get it?). If you've seen the show you'll know that it turned out more 'L&G' than 'L&P', but if you like ginger beer you'll love this! Both of these recipes work, but if you have 48 hours to wait for the bottle-fermented version I really think it's worth the wait.

L&V Bottle Fermented

Energy KJs	Protein	Total fat
624	**.8g**	**.2g**

Saturated fat	Carbohydrate	Sodium
.04g	**33g**	**9mg**

L&V in a Hurry

Energy KJs	Protein	Total fat
875	**.5g**	**.1g**

Saturated fat	Carbohydrate	Sodium
0g	**50g**	**17mg**

L&V

L&V in a hurry
MAKES 8 DRINKS

GINGER JUICE

large knob ginger, peeled

L&V

3 lemons, rind removed and juiced

2 oranges, rind removed and juiced

1 teaspoon citric acid

1 tablespoon ginger juice

1 cup honey

2 cups water

10 drops bitters

FOR THE GINGER JUICE

1. Grate ginger onto two layers of muslin.
2. Squeeze juice through muslin into a bowl.

FOR THE L&V

1. Mix lemon and orange juice, citric acid and ginger juice together.
2. Place honey and water in a saucepan and bring to a simmer. Stir bitters and juice mixture into the honey mixture and simmer to make a syrup.
3. Remove from heat and cool.
4. Pour ¼ cup syrup into each glass over ice, and top with sparkling water.

L&V bottle fermented
MAKES APPROXIMATELY 1 LITRE

100ml honey

200ml water

3 lemons, rind removed and juiced

2 oranges, rind removed and juiced

1 tablespoon ginger juice

10 drops bitters

600ml water

25 granules sweet wine yeast

1. Place honey and 100ml water in a saucepan and bring to a simmer. Add remaining ingredients and mix.
2. Pour into a strong, clean 1 litre bottle with a screw cap. Store in a dark, warm place for 48 hours only.

Serve, undoing the cap gently to slowly release the pressure.

This was a really tough challenge and a lot of work went into this off-camera, trying to perfect it as we got closer to game day. I just couldn't get the colour right! In the end the people at Waiheke's famous Onetangi Races absolutely loved it. It's well worth trying and is a really refreshing drink for a summer's day.

Energy KJs	Protein	Total fat
280	**.1g**	**0g**

Saturated fat	Carbohydrate	Sodium
0g	**16g**	**3mg**

mike's moreish cola

MAKES APPROXIMATELY 1.5 LITRES

2 cups water
zest of 2 oranges
zest of 1 lime
zest of 1 lemon
⅛ teaspoon cinnamon
⅛ teaspoon freshly grated nutmeg
1 star anise
½ teaspoon lavender flowers
2 teaspoons minced ginger
¼ teaspoon citric acid
150ml boiling water
1 tablespoon instant coffee
150ml water
1 tablespoon brown sugar
1 tablespoon molasses
2 cups honey

1. Place 2 cups water, orange, lime and lemon zests, cinnamon, nutmeg, star anise, lavender, ginger and citric acid in a large saucepan and simmer for 20 minutes. Cool then strain through two layers of cheesecloth.
2. Mix boiling water and instant coffee together and chill in refrigerator.
3. Place 150ml water and brown sugar in another pan. Bring to the boil and simmer to caramelise. As spits of caramel form on the side of the pan, use a pastry brush and water to keep the sides clean. When caramel darkens, carefully add the cooled coffee.
4. Stir molasses and honey into strained citrus water, followed by the coffee caramel. Remove from heat and cool. Refrigerate after 15 minutes.

To serve, ladle cola syrup over ice in a large glass. Top with soda water.

This just looks awesome. It's bright, bright orange! Along with the vibrant colour it tastes great and has no added sugar at all. The citric acid just adds a little bit of tartness, but if you don't have it just leave it out.

Energy KJs	Protein	Total fat
371	**2g**	**.4g**

Saturated fat	Carbohydrate	Sodium
.08g	**20g**	**35mg**

mike's audacious orange drink

MAKES 4 LITRES

1 litre freshly juiced orange juice

1 litre freshly juiced blood orange juice

2 litres freshly juiced carrot juice

1 tablespoon citric acid

1. Combine all ingredients and carbonate carefully and slowly through a Soda Stream.

These look really fantastic layered like this but if you wanted to you could just make your smoothie out of one of the recipe variations. I served these little retro beauties at the Puhoi Axe-Men Carnival, and to my surprise they were the biggest hit of the day, selling out in just a few hours.

Energy KJs	Protein	Total fat
948	**7g**	**2g**

Saturated fat	Carbohydrate	Sodium
.6g	**47g**	**57mg**

Traffic light smoothies

MAKES 8

GREEN
1 dessertspoon spirulina powder

2 bananas, peeled

2 apples, cored

1 cup low-fat yoghurt

ORANGE
½ cup orange juice

2 bananas, peeled

2 nectarines, stones removed

1 tablespoon honey

1 cup low-fat yoghurt

RED
2 cups strawberries, hulled

1 cup frozen raspberries or mixed berries

1 dessertspoon honey

2 bananas, peeled

1 cup low-fat yoghurt

1. Blitz all ingredients for each different colour smoothie separately in a blender, and pour each into a jug. Chill.
2. Carefully pour each layer over the back of a spoon into glasses.

Essentials

Tasty, handy bits and bobs to make your meals perfect!

Garlic oil

½ cup canola oil
10 cloves garlic, whole

Heat canola oil and add garlic cloves, including skin.
    Heat to simmer then remove from heat and leave to infuse for 15 minutes.
    Strain and discard garlic.
    Store in a glass jar.

Balsamic reduction

200g brown sugar
400ml balsamic vinegar

Place sugar and vinegar in a heavy-based saucepan. Bring to the boil, reduce heat and simmer until it is a thick consistency when cooled. (Check by cooling a little on a plate in refrigerator.)
    Store in a jar or bottle in refrigerator.

Rocket oil

1 handful rocket
1 tablespoon white wine
⅓ cup olive oil
⅓ cup avocado oil
salt and white pepper to taste

Blanch rocket and refresh in iced water. Drain, and remove as much water as possible by squeezing gently in a clean tea towel.
    Place blanched rocket in a food processor and pulse quickly so rocket does not heat and discolour. Add wine, olive oil, avocado oil, salt and pepper and continue to process for about 2 minutes. Adjust seasoning and pour through a clean muslin cloth. Discard solids.
    Store in a jar in refrigerator.

Salsa verde

½ cup basil, chopped
½ cup Italian parsley, chopped
2 tablespoons baby capers, drained and chopped
1 clove garlic, crushed
zest and juice of 1 lemon
2 tablespoons olive oil
2 tablespoons finely grated Parmesan
2 tablespoons avocado oil
salt and freshly ground black pepper to taste

Place basil, parsley, capers, garlic and lemon zest into a bowl. Add enough olive oil to make the mixture wet. Add Parmesan, remaining olive oil, avocado oil and lemon juice to taste. Season with salt and pepper.
    Store in a jar in refrigerator.

Onion jam

2 onions, peeled and sliced
1 teaspoon olive oil
2 tablespoons red wine vinegar
2 tablespoons brown sugar

Heat a heavy-based frying pan. Cook onion slowly in oil until transparent. Add vinegar and sugar and cook until all liquid has dissolved.

Raisin chutney

4 large tomatoes, chopped
1 cup raisins, soaked in water for 1–2 hours then drained
1 teaspoon brown sugar
¼ fennel bulb, finely diced
4 tablespoons cider vinegar
¼ teaspoon nutmeg
pinch salt
pepper to taste

Place all ingredients in a heavy-based saucepan. Bring to the boil then reduce heat. Simmer for about 30 minutes until thick.
    Mash chutney with a fork, then transfer to a bowl, cover and chill until required.

Pickled fennel

1½ cups white wine vinegar
½ cup sugar
1 star anise
1 bulb fennel, finely sliced on a Japanese turning machine

Bring vinegar, sugar and star anise to the boil in a saucepan. Remove from heat. Add fennel and allow to cool in liquid.
Store in refrigerator.

Kumara purée

4 golden kumara
2 tablespoons olive oil
1 teaspoon flaky salt

Preheat oven to 180°C.
Rub oil onto outside of kumara and sprinkle with salt. Place in a baking dish.
Roast for about 40 minutes or until soft.
Scoop out flesh and pass through a sieve.

Aubergine pickle

2 eggplant, peeled and cut into small dice
2 tablespoons olive oil
3 tomatoes, diced
2 tablespoons dried cranberries
2 tablespoons sunflower seeds
1 teaspoon Food Truck curry powder (see Essentials, page 162)
¼ cup water
pinch salt
freshly ground black pepper to taste

Heat a heavy-based frying pan. Sauté eggplant in olive oil. Add remaining ingredients except seasoning and cook until liquid has evaporated.
Blend with a stick blender or transfer to a food processor and blend until smooth. Season to taste with salt and pepper.

Pea pesto

125g frozen peas, boiled, drained and crushed
2 tablespoons chopped parsley
½ tablespoon Dijon mustard
1 large shallot, finely diced
2 tablespoons avocado oil

Mix together all ingredients.
   Store in refrigerator.

Chow chow

500g mixed vegetables, diced: cauliflower florets, deseeded cucumber,
   celery, carrots, baby onions
1 teaspoon sea salt
2 cups water
¹/₃ cup honey
½ teaspoon turmeric
½ teaspoon mustard seeds
½ teaspoon celery seeds
1½ cups cider vinegar
2 tablespoons cornflour
4 tablespoons water

Place diced vegetables in a large bowl. Add salt and water. Cover and let
stand overnight in refrigerator.
   Next day, place vegetables and water in a large saucepan, bring slowly to
the boil and simmer for 1 minute. Drain well.
   In another saucepan, combine honey, turmeric, mustard and celery
seeds and vinegar.
   Slowly bring to the boil, stirring constantly, then simmer for a few
minutes.
   Mix cornflour and water together and add to sauce to thicken.
   Add sauce to hot vegetables and stir together well.
   Pour into sterilised jars to store.

VARIATION: APPLE CHOW CHOW
Add 1 peeled and diced apple after combining sauce with hot vegetables.
Stir through.

El Speciale Sauce

GREEN SALSA

3 green chillies, halved and deseeded
1 tomato, roughly chopped
2 cloves garlic, peeled and roughly chopped
pinch salt
7 canned tomatillos, drained and chopped
½ cup coriander leaves

Blend together chillies, tomato, garlic and salt in a food processor. Add tomatillos and coriander and pulse.

RED SALSA

4 tomatoes, skinned, deseeded and finely chopped
½ onion, finely sliced
2 cloves garlic, peeled
10 red chillies, halved and deseeded
pinch salt
1 avocado, diced

Heat a heavy-based frying pan. Cook tomatoes, onion and garlic until just coloured. Transfer to a food processor. Lightly brown chillies in the same pan and add to the food processor with salt. Blend ingredients together.

FOR THE SAUCE

Mix green and red salsa together, then gently fold in the avocado.

Tomato sauce

300g beefsteak tomatoes, cut in half horizontally
5 cloves garlic, peeled
20g each rosemary, thyme, basil and parsley leaves
pinch sea salt
1 tablespoon olive oil
1 handful each fresh basil and parsley

Preheat oven to 100°C. Spray an oven tray with oil. Arrange tomato halves on oven tray. Sprinkle over garlic, rosemary, thyme, basil and parsley and a small amount of sea salt. Place in preheated oven and leave to cook and dry for 8 hours. Remove herbs. Transfer tomatoes to a blender, add olive oil and fresh basil and parsley, and purée.

Roasted Portobello mushrooms

6 Portobello mushrooms, peeled
1 tablespoon olive oil
salt and pepper to taste

Preheat oven to 180°C. Place mushrooms, gills up, on a baking tray. Sprinkle with olive oil and salt and pepper. Bake for 10 minutes or until tender.

Spiced tomatoes

6 large tomatoes, cut in half
2 sprigs rosemary
2 tablespoons chopped thyme
4 cloves garlic, smashed
1 teaspoon flaky salt
¼ teaspoon cracked pepper
2 tablespoons olive oil
1 tablespoon sugar
pinch chilli powder

Preheat oven to 180°C. Place tomatoes in a baking dish. Add rosemary, thyme, garlic, salt and pepper and roast for 20–30 minutes. Remove from oven and discard herbs and garlic. Place tomatoes in a blender, add olive oil, sugar and chilli powder and blitz until smooth. Place in a saucepan and reduce by about half, until thick.

Red pepper salad & olives

4 red peppers
1 teaspoon oil
pinch salt
2 tablespoons Kalamata olives
6 cloves garlic, roasted
zest of 1 lemon
1 tablespoon chopped parsley
1 teaspoon capers
2 tablespoons olive oil

Rub peppers with oil and salt and chargrill over an open flame. Place in a bowl, cover with plastic wrap and leave to steam and cool. Peel, remove seeds and slice into thin strips. Add remaining ingredients and mix together.

Baked potatoes

4 large Agria potatoes
rice bran oil spray
8 tablespoons Mike's baked beans (see below)
4 eggs
white pepper

Preheat oven to 180°C.
Lightly spray skin of potatoes with oil and place in a baking dish.
Cook potatoes in preheated oven for about 30 minutes or until soft. Remove potatoes from oven and cool.
Increase oven temperature to 200°C.
Slice off top third of each potato and hollow out the larger section, leaving 5mm of potato flesh on the skin. Set aside potato flesh.
Spoon 1 tablespoon of baked beans into each potato case. Break in 1 raw egg then top with another tablespoon of baked beans. Sprinkle removed potato flesh over top and spray with oil. Season with white pepper.
Return to oven and bake for 15 minutes until golden.

Mike's baked beans

3 slices pancetta (optional)
1 onion, diced
4 cloves garlic, crushed
4 tomatoes, diced
1 tablespoon tomato purée
2 teaspoon dried thyme or fresh thyme leaves
2 tablespoon Dijon mustard
2 tablespoon brown sugar
2 cups water
1 x 400g can chickpeas, drained and rinsed
1 x 400g can red kidney beans, drained and rinsed
1 x 400g can borlotti beans, drained and rinsed
1 x 400g can haricot beans, drained and rinsed
pinch salt
white pepper to taste

Sauté pancetta in a large heavy-based saucepan. Add onion and garlic and cook until transparent. Add tomatoes, tomato purée, thyme, mustard, brown sugar and water and stir well. Add beans and salt and pepper and cook for about 10–20 minutes until thoroughly heated and sauce is thick.

Bacon and egg wrap

Here's a fabulous alternative to the good old bacon and egg pie. It's low fat and looks so beautiful when you slice into it. When I sold it to the axe-men at Puhoi, it went down a treat.

BROAD BEAN SALSA

1 teaspoon rice bran oil

1 leek, white part only, finely sliced

2 handfuls spinach, blanched, drained and squeezed dry

½ cup broad beans, blanched and podded

½ cup frozen peas, blanched

Heat oil in a frying pan, add leek and cook until soft.

Place cooked leek in a bowl, add remaining ingredients and toss together.

TO ASSEMBLE

1 wholemeal tortilla

2 tablespoons broad bean salsa

2 rashers lean bacon, cooked and sliced

2 poached eggs

Heat a sandwich press.

Lay tortilla on a chopping board. Spread with salsa and top with bacon. Place eggs on top and roll up tightly.

Cook in hot sandwich press for 2–3 minutes. Slice in half to serve.

Citrus mash

500g boiling potatoes, peeled and diced

pinch salt

½ cup low-fat milk

zest of ½ lemon

Place potatoes and salt in a saucepan and cover with water. Bring to the boil, reduce heat and simmer for about 10 minutes.

Pour milk into a small saucepan and add lemon zest. Bring to the boil, reduce heat and simmer for 3 minutes. Remove from heat.

Drain potatoes. Add milk mixture and mash.

Coleslaw

COLESLAW

½ cup finely shredded red cabbage

½ cup finely shredded green cabbage

1 carrot, peeled and grated

½ bulb fennel, finely sliced and soaked in lemon water for
 5 minutes

¼ red onion, finely sliced

1 tablespoon chopped, toasted walnuts

DRESSING

1 egg yolk

juice of ½ a lemon

pinch salt

pinch sugar

4 tablespoons olive oil

Put coleslaw ingredients in a bowl and mix.

Place dressing ingredients in a screw-top jar and shake to combine.

Drizzle half the dressing over coleslaw and toss to combine. Remaining dressing can be stored in refrigerator.

Brussels slaw

SLAW

12 Brussels sprouts, trimmed and finely sliced

3 carrots, peeled and finely sliced

DRESSING

3 tablespoons red wine vinegar

1 tablespoon honey

4 tablespoons avocado oil

pinch salt

white pepper to taste

Mix slaw ingredients together. Mix all dressing ingredients together. Dress slaw.

VARIATION: BEAN AND BRUSSELS SLAW

Add 18 green beans, blanched and sliced in half lengthwise, to slaw.

Charred summer salad

2 red peppers
3 courgettes, cut lengthwise into 3mm thick slices
1 red onion, sliced into 12 wedges
1 eggplant, cut into 3mm thick slices
salt and pepper to taste
¼ cup olive oil

Chargrill peppers following method in red pepper salad recipe on page 153.

Heat a ridged frying pan or barbecue to hot.

Toss courgettes, onion and eggplant with salt, pepper and olive oil. Place vegetables in pan or on barbecue and grill until charred.

Place in a bowl, add sliced red peppers and toss.

Naan bread

You can pat or slap the dough to form the elongated shape. It's fun trying to make the traditional slap sound.

1 cup white all-purpose flour
1 cup wholemeal flour
¾ teaspoon baking powder
pinch baking soda
¼ teaspoon salt
1 teaspoon sugar
½ cup warm milk
½ cup yoghurt
1 cup mung beans

Sieve flours, baking powder, baking soda and salt together twice. Add wholemeal grains left in the sieve back into bowl. Place dry ingredients on a clean work surface and make a well in the centre. Add sugar, milk and yoghurt and with your hands slowly combine to form a soft dough. Place in a bowl, cover with a damp cloth and let it rest for 2 hours.

Preheat a pizza cooker until hot or a barbecue plate until very hot.

After resting, add mung beans and knead dough gently for 2 minutes.

Dust your working surface with some flour. Pinch off a large lemon-sized piece of dough and roll between two pieces of greaseproof paper into an elongated oval shape.

Place on base of hot pizza cooker, cover with a lid, and cook for 40–45 seconds on high. Alternatively place in preheated oven at 220°C for 90 seconds.

Turn and cook the other side.

Brown rice

BOUQUET GARNI
1 teaspoon fennel seeds
1 teaspoon coriander seeds
1 teaspoon black peppercorns
1–2 bay leaves

Wrap whole spices in a piece of kitchen cloth or muslin and tie the top.

RICE
2 cups brown basmati rice, washed
1 lemon, halved
1 bouquet garni

Place brown rice, lemon and bouquet garni in a saucepan. Pour in enough water to come 2.5cm above rice. Bring to the boil, reduce heat, cover and simmer for 10 minutes.

Turn off element, leave lid on and leave on element for about 5 minutes. Remove lid, and run fork through rice to separate grains.

Food Truck garam masala

1 tablespoon coriander seeds
1 tablespoon cumin seeds
1 tablespoon cardamom pods
1 tablespoon fennel seeds
1 tablespoon whole cloves
1 tablespoon broken cinnamon quill

Preheat oven to 200°C.

Place all ingredients on a baking tray and roast until golden and fragrant. Transfer to a mortar and pestle and grind until smooth.

Food Truck curry powder

1 x quantity Food Truck garam masala
1 teaspoon ground turmeric
1 teaspoon mild chilli powder or paprika

Mix all ingredients together. Store in an airtight container.

Lemonade

2 tablespoons lemon juice
2 tablespoons runny honey
1 litre water
4 sprigs fresh mint

Put lemon juice and honey in a saucepan. Bring to a simmer, remove from heat and cool. Place water in Soda Stream and make into soda water.

Place ice in tall glasses, add 2 tablespoons of lemon syrup to each and top with soda water. Garnish with mint sprigs.

Ice-cream cones

MAKES 6

50g butter
50g castor sugar
2 egg whites, beaten
50g flour
1½ tablespoons sesame seeds
1 tablespoon chia seeds
1½ tablespoons black sesame seeds

Preheat oven to 160°C. Line a baking tray with baking paper.

Cream butter and sugar until pale and creamy. Fold in egg whites, followed by flour, then mix in seeds. The mixture will be quite sticky.

On the lined baking tray, spread the mixture over six circular stencil moulds that you have cut from a plastic ice-cream container lid (or similar) to about the circumference of a teacup saucer. Run a knife over the dough so it is no higher than the height of the plastic. This is to ensure a consistent thickness so the dough will bake evenly. Refrigerate for 1 hour.

Remove the stencil and place tray in preheated oven to bake for 4 minutes. Mould into cone shapes while still warm and malleable.

Sherbet

4 tablespoons freeze-dried fruit powder (available at specialty food stores), any flavour
5 teaspoons baking soda
10 teaspoons icing sugar, sifted
2½ teaspoons citric acid

Mix all ingredients together and store in an airtight container.

A word from the Heart Foundation

The Heart Foundation is New Zealand's heart health charity. Since 1968, we have been active in our communities supporting people with heart disease, working alongside health professionals, funding pioneering research, connecting with our schools, and advocating for those at risk. Over the last 40 years, deaths from heart disease have halved, yet this disease remains New Zealand's single biggest killer. It shuts down one heart every 90 minutes — 16 lives needlessly lost every day. Our work is not done yet.

People say 'it's the little things that make the biggest difference', and that's true of all the little choices we're faced with in our daily lives. We are deeply passionate about encouraging and equipping people with knowledge and tools to make positive lifestyle changes — making those little choices that promise vitality, joy and fulfillment. They affect our health, our outlook on life, and lift us to make the most of life and play our part in the lives of others near to us.

It's why we work alongside people like Mike and the Food Truck. His determination to inspire all Kiwis to make choices towards a healthier future can make all the difference. Please visit www.heartfoundation.org.nz for motivating resources on how to spot and grab hold of little, positive, everyday lifestyle changes so we can all achieve our hopes and dreams and fulfill our lifetime.

Healthy options

There are lots of ways you can achieve the flavour and taste of takeaway-style food at home — and indeed with all your cooking — without piling on the fat, the sugar and the salt.

To reduce salt use

- In general, reduce the amount of salt used but if using it, make sure it is *iodised*. To add flavour use herbs, spices, lemon juice and pepper in place of salt.
- Make sauces with low-salt stocks, water, fruit juice, low-fat milk and yoghurt. Thickening with flour, cornflour or arrowroot will reduce fat use too.
- Use low-salt varieties of soy, fish, oyster and other Asian sauces, and in general *reduce* the amount used.
- Instead of stock cubes and commercially made stocks use *home-made* stock and reduced vegetable cooking water.
- Use canned vegetable varieties that have no added salt.
- Use low-salt varieties of peanut butter in place of regular peanut butter.

To get more fibre

- Instead of white flour use wholemeal flour or half white and half wholemeal.
- *Replace* white bread with wholemeal pita bread or wholegrain bread, and use wholemeal breadcrumbs in place of white.
- To thicken and extend braises and stews, add rice, barley, oats or red lentils.
- Use wholemeal pasta and brown rice *instead of* pasta and white rice.
- Peel vegetables and fruits only when necessary.

To use less sugar

- *Instead of* regular canned fruit use canned fruit in light syrup, non-sweetened or canned in its own juice.
- Instead of icing a cake, dust it with icing sugar, *or use* a layer of fresh berries on top. Replace cream-cheese icing with ricotta, yoghurt and honey, or make it with lite cream cheese.

- *Reduce the use of* sugar, honey and golden syrup and substitute natural fruit, fruit purée or fruit juice as sweeteners.
- Instead of regular yoghurt use natural or unsweetened yoghurt.
- Stew fruit in a little water only, with no added sugar.

Watch the type of fat used

- Use margarine, table spreads or oil *rather than* butter.
- Hummus, mashed avocado, mayonnaise, tahini or pesto also *make great alternatives* to butter on bread.
- When making pancakes, pikelets or fritters, spray the surface of your pan *sparingly* with cooking spray.
- Instead of shortening and lard use margarine or vegetable oil.
- Rather than cheddar cheese *substitute a lower fat* cheese, e.g. Edam or Mozzarella. Add extra flavour with a small amount of mustard.
- *Replace* full-fat soft cheese, sour cream or yoghurt with lower fat varieties such as cottage cheese, ricotta, quark or lite cream cheese.
- *Instead* of full-fat milk use low-fat skim milk or trim milk (1.5% fat or less).
- Use reduced fat cream if it doesn't require whipping; or replace with low-fat natural yoghurt or Greek yoghurt; or if suitable, use custard instead.
- Instead of full-fat coconut cream or coconut milk use a lite version; or lite evaporated milk with coconut essence; or low-fat yoghurt mixed with *small amounts* of desiccated coconut diluted with low-fat milk.
- Toast pita bread chunks or tortilla wraps cut to size, or bake slices of French bread in the oven until crispy to serve with dips instead of chips and crisps.
- Instead of regular mayonnaise and salad dressings use reduced fat varieties and/or dilute with low-fat yoghurt or milk.

- Choose *lean cuts of meat* and trim off visible fat before cooking.
- When cooking meat, grill, stew, bake or roast on a rack, with no added fat.
- Use only very small amounts of salami and bacon to flavour dishes. This adds less salt too.
- If cooking sausages or sausage meat, *reduce the amount used* and extend with rice, pasta, legumes or vegetables. If using pre-cooked sausages, choose lower fat varieties.
- When cooking fish, poach, grill, microwave or steam rather than deep-frying. Baked crumbed fish has far less fat than deep-fried battered fish.
- Use fish canned in water rather than oil or brine. It contains less salt too!
- When cooking vegetables, steam, boil or microwave in a little water, avoiding overcooking. Sauté, bake or stir-fry by brushing the pan with a small amount of oil, or use an oil spray then add a little water or fruit juice.
- *Bake, microwave or mash* potatoes rather than roasting in animal fat or deep-frying. Mash with low-fat milk or lite evaporated milk, and a small amount of light margarine. If needed, add extra flavour with mustard, horseradish, herbs or caramelised onion.
- Instead of creamy sauces use tomato-based sauces and use *low-fat* milk or *lite* margarine in white sauces.

Cooking methods

Baking

- Oven-bake foods, without adding fat.
- Replace butter in baking recipes with a healthy oil, margarine or spread. (Spreads contain more water than butter or margarine, so choose a variety that has at least 60 per cent fat when substituting for butter.)
- Use fruit purée as a replacement for half the butter or margarine.
- Use silicone sheets or baking paper instead of greasing dishes with butter or cooking spray.

Pan-frying and stir-frying

- Spray the pan with an oil spray instead of using oil or butter.
- Choose vegetable oils with a higher smoke point for frying such as sunflower, soybean, canola or rice bran.

Deep-frying

- Deep-frying is not recommended because it produces food that is especially high in energy.
- Many foods that are traditionally deep-fried, such as chips, can be oven-baked for a healthier result.

Roasting

- Use a rack when roasting meat and lightly spray baking trays with a little oil when roasting vegetables.

Stews and braises

- Use milk in place of cream, lite coconut milk instead of coconut cream and low-salt stocks.

Index

The People Who made This Book

Mike

Mike Van de Elzen and his wife Belinda established the famous Auckland neighbourhood restaurant Molten, in Mount Eden, eight years ago. Molten went on to win many restaurant awards, and in 2011 Mike published his first book, The Molten Cookbook, to rave reviews.

Babiche

Babiche Martens is a photographer at the New Zealand Herald and her great photos regularly appear in the Herald's 'Viva' supplement. She also took all the photos for The Molten Cookbook. www.babichemartens.com

Nick

Nick Ward and James Anderson own and operate the television production company Two Heads. The Food Truck is their first primetime series for TVNZ. www.twoheads.co.nz

Beddy

OK, she's not really a person but we just had to include the truck, who we fondly call Beddy. She's a 1970 Bedford J1. Before we got her, Charlie's juice used her as a promotional truck, and before that she belonged to Wellington chef Martin Bosley, who bought her as a wreck on Trade Me. The rest is culinary history.

ACKNOWLEDGEMENTS

Thanks heaps to the guys at Two Heads, Nick and James, for giving me the keys to the Food Truck and thanks to TVNZ for screening the two series of the show. Thanks to the wonderful Babiche Martens, with whom I had such a good time taking the amazing recipe photos. Thanks to the good people at the New Zealand Heart Foundation for their interest and support, especially Pip Duncan, who wrote down my rambling ingredients lists and methods and turned them into recipes. Thanks to my publisher, Random House. Thanks to all the pie-makers, short-order cooks and chefs who let me in on their trade secrets. Thanks to my wife Belinda and one-year-old daughter Hazel, who never complained when I drove off in the Food Truck on a sunny weekend day to roam the countryside selling my food when I could have been at home with them. But most of all, thanks to all the Kiwis who rolled up to the truck and bought my food and told me it was great. You guys are the best!

Mike